Zoroaster's Children

Zoroaster's Children

AND OTHER TRAVELS

Marius Kociejowski

BIBLIOASIS
WINDSOR, ONTARIO

FIRST EDITION

Library and Archives Canada Cataloguing in Publication

Kociejowski, Marius, author
    Zoroaster's children and other travels / Marius Kociejowski. Essays.

Issued in print and electronic formats.
ISBN 978-1-77196-044-1 (paperback).--ISBN 978-1-77196-045-8 (ebook)
    1. Kociejowski, Marius--Travel. I. Title.

PS8571.O64Z43 2015   C814'.54   C2015-903733-6
                                               C2015-903734-4

Edited by Dan Wells
Copy-edited by Allana Amlin
Typeset and designed by Chris Andrechek

Published with the generous assistance of the Canada Council for the Arts and the Ontario Arts Council. Biblioasis also acknowledges the support of the Government of Canada through the Canada Book Fund and the Government of Ontario through the Ontario Book Publishing Tax Credit.

PRINTED AND BOUND IN CANADA

Contents

for Bobbie
silent companion of some of these travels

Some Places I've Been To

I'VE BEEN READING HERMIONE EYRE's *Viper Wine* (Jonathan Cape, 2014). The writing dazzles, and, at times, with its many stretches of Jacobean pastiche, almost too much so. A woman I know won't go near the book for its virtuosic glare. The novel is set in 1632 with fanciful intrusions, sometimes to extraordinary effect, from the present day, the arrival of an acid cloud above London being one such instance. I'd made the mistake of mentioning to my friend that David Bowie makes a fleeting appearance. Orlando Gibbons, I could hear her think, come hither. It's probably too late to invite her to sample the following passage:

> So soft and suggestible are we, she thought—men and women both—and there is so much about us still unknown, and yet people adventure into foreign lands. I would sooner go to the edge of a woman's tear duct, she thought, as to the great Cataracts of the Nile, to know the nerves behind a flayed man's face, before I knew Madagascar, or the moon.

Actually, ostrich-plumed hats off to her, Miss Eyre's is a marvellous book, and the words I quote above are yet another instance of how certain works, or even single passages in them, can so neatly fall into place. I had been contemplating how

1

best to begin an essay that is designed to segue into the other pieces in this book and her words come at just the right time. I think that with respect to my own geographical coordinates I stand midway between a woman's tear duct and the waning moon.

I have been described, though not often, as a travel writer, an appellation that vaguely embarrasses me. A couple of books, which sit in the travel sections of bookshops, have had the effect of making me into what I may not be. I do not have the means to be a traveller or to be able to just pick up and go. Also I'm idle. Oblomov outstrips me. I'm not a tourist either. A tourist moves inside a bubble; a traveller forgoes the safety of that bubble. I am sufficiently enough of a coward to not go risking my hide, but then again, I have gone where many think it folly to do so. There have been instances. Somebody I know says he'd never go anywhere with me. I'm reckless in his eyes. But does this make me a traveller? Then again, who among us is *not* a traveller, stumbling upon vortexes, which, like certain dreams we have, we try later to give meaning to? Are we not travellers from the day we are born? And are we not at risk all the time? Yet the ease with which we can go places, even dangerous ones, is such that we need to rethink the very notion of what it is to travel. There is nowhere on the planet one can't get to, and to a fair degree this has made redundant the idea of a narrative, and so I think it has become incumbent upon authors to write not so much about *getting to* a place as in being able to write *out of it*. A traveller goes with what he has, which, one hopes, includes a fair measure of knowledge but which is useful only to the degree that same knowledge does not cloud what is actually in front of his eyes.

The travel writers I know are almost always on the move, they wear exotic clothes, they have survived snake bite, and they speak the more remote dialects of already impenetrable languages. One of them, a most fascinating figure, was recently spotted heading a tour of the brave on the North West Frontier and seemingly impervious to the world's jittery state. There's a book he appears to be in no hurry to complete. I'm not so sure he has even begun it. The book may be *him alone*. One day his name will grace a school of studies. If there's a desire in me to separate myself from the travel writing crowd, it is not that I disparage the works of those who are in it, for I believe much of the best English prose is to be found in what they produce, but rather because when compared to the coloratura of their lives mine pales. This said, I would sooner sit with them than with a group of poets. (I have been called a poet, too, a label with which I am rather more comfortable because it's so threadbare.) So, why travel writers rather than poets? Simple. While the latter bemoan a world that insufficiently recognises them, the world is what the former most like to describe.

I don't have languages and am quite unable to retain such words and phrases as I have picked up here and there, but then I have met people who do, who converse with ease, who do not pay over the odds for an aubergine, and yet are no wiser to the people whose tongues they speak. Often they will be the first to lay the charge that one cannot get close to the soul of a country without first knowing its language. The curious thing is that those who say so tend not to be writers. All the same, it's difficult to argue with them. The best travel writers speak the lingo, of course, and I shall be forever in awe of them. Wilfred Thesiger spoke fluent Arabic. I met him once. So nervous I was in the presence of this greatest of twentieth-century travellers all I could think to ask him was the identity of some birds that years before I'd seen flying in extraordinary formation above the Sahara. They flew in a constantly shifting pattern too intricate for language to describe. I can see them still, but I can't tell you *what* I see. I made a stab at it with Thesiger. He thought for a minute and said, gruffly, and with great authority, 'Sand birds'. When I mentioned this to someone who knew him the response was, 'Oh, Wilfred knows bugger all about birds.' While I am fully aware of my linguistic handicap, which admittedly is a serious one, and am ornithologically challenged (though not as badly as some people), I would suggest that there are ways by which one might compensate a little.

Mind you, I've been extraordinarily lucky: I could not have written my two books on Syria without the help of a couple of people, Arabs both, whose mastery of the English language and their quickness of mind were such that they could translate with the rapidity of a UN interpreter and at the same time preserve the nuances, and, most importantly, the humour, of the original. The incredible thing is that they were not academics but picked up English mostly by serendipity, somewhere between a stack of movie magazines and the marketplace. Even if I spoke Arabic passably well, I doubt I'd be able to suck the juice from the pomegranate.[1] What I mean by this is my getting at the deeper meaning seeded inside language. What greatly helped me is that my Arab friends were willing to subscribe to my sometimes batty schemes. I'd be nowhere without them, still splashing about in the shallows, spouting generalities. Generality, and not, as some like to say, 'preconceived notions', is the true enemy of one's deeper enquiries into human nature.

Empathy, I place empathy above language. A writer who lacks it is not one who greatly interests me. I disqualify Lawrence Durrell from my boudoir for describing the Egyptian poor as 'apes in nightgowns' and this was a writer, a poet no less, who had a tremendous gift for describing locale. The empathy which informs Alberto Denti di Pirajno's *A Cure for Serpents*

---

1   I did see a woman in Iran deflate a pomegranate in this manner. She made a small hole in the surface, put her mouth to it, and with astounding, though gentle, power siphoned its juices in the space of about a minute. She challenged me to do the same, with another pomegranate. I got nowhere, but then I could never blow balloons either.

(1955), one of my favourite travelogues, is wholly absent from his subsequent work and yet I cling to the first book whereas Durrell I exclude whole and it's because I think the latter, in the space of only three words, so fully exposes his inner core. Voices aplenty tell me that when it comes to talk of literature a moral stance is untenable and that one must reach critically beyond one's own distaste. So be it. Flawed though my position may be, or, worse still, unfashionable, what I hope to find in another's work is an inviolable sense of justice, such as one finds throughout the writings of Robert Louis Stevenson, most powerfully in his *Father Damien: An Open Letter to the Reverend Doctor Hyde of Honolulu* (1890). There he displays empathy for a man whose faith he could not share.[2] Also I hold that if one looks deeply enough into another man's soul the closer one will come to the world he inhabits, and, for me, this holds doubly true for those people who inhabit the margins of, or who are actually outside, society for they are the ones who point towards a middle ground of conformity that will not contain them. I wade through negatives in order to make a point but this is the way I work and I make no apologies for it: I travel more through people than I do through places.

And while I'm at it, and I'm thinking only of the more tedious travel narratives, I don't want to hear about stomach cramps, diarrhoea, bad plumbing, petty thieves, and people with funny voices, nor do I want to bide my time with those who spread themselves over the landscape unless what is being spread is of greater interest than the slice of planet they describe. Allah spare us from 'travellers' tales'. They are not always escapable, but one must know when to avoid them. Oh, and I'd have to include in my catalogue of avoidance

---

2   One of the many pleasurable moments afforded to me as an antiquarian bookseller was when Patti Smith came into the shop one day and was perusing the shelves and she gasped, "Oh, my favourite author!" It was only after she came to the desk with a small volume of Stevenson in her hand that I decided I would attend her next concert. It was in Brighton and she did not disappoint there either.

nearly all the journals of nineteenth- and early twentieth-century missionary's wives. I've gone through a good many of them and feel that a decent percentage of their authors, most of them probably bored out of their wits, ought to have been cannibalised along with their becollared husbands. Such are my gripes, ignore them. One should not stand too much in the way of what one sees. If, as some people have remarked, I am something of an absentee from my own prose, I hope it is with the consequence that what I write are deeply personal accounts if only by virtue of what I choose to write about. I am not saying this ought to apply to others writing in the genre, some of whom are absolute masters when rendering a sense of place, but only to point out I have my own approach to things, without which I'd be in Palookaville.

SOME MONTHS AGO, I awoke from a dream which, as dreams often do, melted away before I could bottle even a drop of it. I did taste of its substance however. A desperate voice in my head shouted *where are they*? All day the question clung to me, with slight permutations. 'Where are they *now*?' Maybe it was not a dream at all but a darting thought of no more than a couple of seconds' duration snagged on the borderline between sleep and awakening. The radio was on and so perhaps something on the news had seeped into me. The news had been awfully grim with barely a day gone by that did not bring word of yet another massacre. There is always horror somewhere, but this was in a country I knew and loved, and which at dark moments is now beyond the reach of my knowledge and love. I feel too angry for love or so I say. *So I say.* I'm not sure if anything makes sense anymore. Words splutter on the page. And I now discover this is felt even more deeply by people who are actually from there.

(Bear with me, I must interrupt myself here. Yesterday I walked along the route that takes me to the outdoor market on

North End Road in London, which passes through a favourite spot of mine, the Margravine Cemetery in Hammersmith, which is largely Victorian, many of the gravestones therein tilted at crazy angles as if subject to some subterranean upheaval brought about by restless souls. Yes, one can become awfully fanciful there, especially when walking through a winter mist, the leaves plucked from the trees. Something stopped me in my tracks, an unnatural scar of white against the grey of one of the tombstones. I saw another flash of white and then another. The heads of many of the stone angels had been smashed away. I wonder if I can bear to go that way anymore. The search is on for a man believed to be acting alone and who has been in other cemeteries, vandalising the stones. It seems to me that whatever insensitivity could allow for the destruction of those angels' heads could just as easily allow for the removal of human ones. I am further put in mind of what was done three years ago to the statue of the blind Syrian poet, Abul 'Ala al-Ma'arri (973–1058) in the village of Maarrat al-Nu'man near Aleppo. The man of the unruly tongue had his head removed and this was even before the emergence in the area of more extreme forces, who decapitate their innocent victims, although what do they care for innocence?)

Where are they, where have they got to?

In 1996 I was at the ruins of the monastery complex of Saint Simeon near Aleppo, where the fifth-century ascetic, Simeon Stylites, stood on a pillar for thirty-seven years. It was my second visit there. Maybe in defiance of authority, or, more inanely, to avoid the bloated admission charge foreigners had to pay, I climbed up the inaccessible side of the mount, and, like a commando in a war movie, ducking low, scrambled across the top of it, over a wire fence, and, on the other side of it, grinning inwardly at some puzzled faces, I made my way into the complex where I paid my dues to cranky Christendom as I'd done a year before. I placed my hand on the stump of the pillar, which, after centuries of pilgrims with small hammers seeking souvenirs, is all that survives of the original edifice. I'll defend Simeon against the cynics. Although I'm no connoisseur of self-mortification I salute him all the same. We need more of his like, who could so wisely, so foolishly, adjudicate, who had, yes, an innate sense of justice. I then fell into conversation with some French tourists who were having a picnic and berating the Syrian wine, which I have to agree is terrible. It pours with the sluggish effluence of cough medicine. At a kiosk not far from the exit I heard a young tourist squabbling over the price of something or other, getting more objectionable by the minute, and then I walked boldly out through the main entrance, past the ticket seller who I could see was trying to register my face. It was a cheap victory but I felt morally superior to the tourist whose voice was now full of expletives. I wished him cheated to the same degree I'd cheated the authorities. Am I petty? One can never be petty enough.

Down below, I found myself at a fork in the road, the main road that led back to Aleppo and a small country road going I knew not where. It was a splendid day for a walk, a slight breeze in the air, and because there were few places in Syria so remote one could not find a way home I took the unknown route. I enjoyed the solitude. A tractor came along, pulling a small wagon with several girls in it of about twelve or thirteen, so pretty in their coloured scarves, standing against the wooden side boards. The driver stopped and signalled to me to get into the wagon. I struggled against a reluctance to break my solitude but when travelling very rarely do I refuse invitations because so often they lead to adventure. I jumped in. At the middle of the wagon floor was a pyramid of pomegranates. They were beautiful in the sunlight and so, too, were the beaming faces of the girls who'd picked them. Syrian children are among the world's loveliest. The girls giggled between themselves and then, their confidence growing, they poked at me, making jokes. After a while, the driver pulled into a village and stopped at which point two of the girls leapt out and, grabbing me by the hands, they pulled me after them, marched me along the street as if I were some kind of human trophy. They took me to their parents' house where, royally treated, I spent the next few hours. I was fed sheep's testicles which, thankfully, were disguised in a spicy sauce, and then the girls' father took me for a walk out of the village and through olive groves. The countryside with its reddish soil, against which the dusty green of the olive trees was most striking, was dotted with Byzantine ruins.

I was in Basofan which I already knew to be a Yezidi village. In Aleppo there had been scurrilous talk of the place and its people. Devil worshippers they were supposed to be. Allegedly Yezidis had an aversion to all sorts of things—they would not wear the colour blue or eat lettuce—which, when I first learned about it, raised a chuckle in me. Once among them, however, I felt reverence for whatever it was that made them the kind and hospitable people they were. I had only to think of those children's faces. I tried to glean from my host what I could about the Yezidi faith. The Yezidis are secretive about their faith and this may be a consequence of their having had to endure centuries of prejudice. I would not have understood the origins or intricacies of their beliefs but I would like to have seen an altar or a shrine, some physical trace. There was one comical interlude: I kept saying the word *Yezidi* in the hope it might open a door for me. After a while the man seemed to get my drift and led me into a room where there was a huge television set, satellite TV as it turned out. *Television*, *Yezidi*: there must have been some kind of aural dance between the sounds of those two words. The man put cushions to either side of me, and the first station he tuned into was from Warsaw. I protested, saying, no, no television please. *Yezidi, Yezidi*. I was asked to spend the night with them and it was with difficulty

I tried to explain I had a friend to meet in Aleppo although in truth there wasn't one. I felt we had already exhausted all possibilities and what I had already was beyond measure.

Slowly it came to me, the import of that dream. It was with the memory of those girls in the wagon that I awoke in a panic, a voice in my head screaming, 'Where are they? Where are those girls?' They would be in their twenties now and the Yezidis are being persecuted as they have never been before, the men being slaughtered by the fanatics of the group calling itself Islamic State, or ISIS or ISIL, the young women raped or carried off into forced marriage with the killers of their husbands, brothers and fathers. *My God, those girls, where are they now?* I had gone narrowly though deeply enough into their world for what had been a happy experience to return, years later, as a nightmare. Maybe this is what makes for a traveller, the deeper absorption of a place and its people. A traveller I am and shall be. A travel writer though? I'm still not sure.

SOMETIMES MY MEMORY of some bit of the world is concentrated in a single human face. Years ago, in October 1973, after the holidaymakers had gone home, my girlfriend and I set up tent in an empty campsite in Greece, snow-capped Mount Olympus in the distance. There's something I love about campsites out of season, their poetical silences. There was a storm that night, of the kind that makes the Aegean Sea such a dangerous place for sailors. It flattened our tent. At first light, maybe because I couldn't deal with my inadequacies as a camper, I began to explore, leaving my good lady to deal with the wreckage. *Suddenly he comes, an elderly man with several golden apples in his hands, offering them to me. The apples are bruised, small brown splotches on them, and the old man's face is grizzled with white.* Were there perhaps only three apples? They might have been the apples Aphrodite gave to Melanion, and which he dropped one by one in order to distract Atalanta so that he might win the race against her and thereby win her hand in marriage. Guido Reni painted the scene, both of them naked, the wind blowing Melanion's single cloth garment in such a way that it covers his privates. Atalanta, what did she do with the apples? Surely, once she was tricked into marriage, she didn't eat them. Maybe she gave them to an elderly man wearing suspenders and a thread-bare shirt, the grizzled custodian of an empty campsite. This man, who now must be some decades dead, proffering golden apples in an empty campsite—the Parthenon, by comparison, sits in the memory like a creased postcard.

I meant to give some kind of abbreviated account of some places I've been to, which are not within the span of this collection. I can't do it. I thought it might be the easiest of all things to write, but no, all that comes into view are mere glimpses. Maybe I should stick to more recent adventures. Some days I go hardly anywhere. Other days I go the few yards it takes me to get to the end of the street and I feel I have covered a good stretch of the world. What I am saying here is that there are days when one's receptors are shut down and others when they are open wide. Let's not forget Xavier de Maistre's 1795 travelogue *A Journey Around My Room* (1795), a parody set in the tradition of the grand travel narrative. What it says to us is that one doesn't have to go very far to get somewhere. What it says, too, is *one must learn to observe*.

Other kinds of journeys are being made. There are the peo-ple I call 'walkers'. They are not walkers such as one encoun-ters in the countryside nor do they have any intellectual design on the cityscape. They walk because they have to. They walk off something inside themselves. Staying put might destroy them. There are two such where I live: one of them wears a woollen tuque, even in summer, and jaywalks across the street opposite our kitchen window from precisely the same point several times a day and comes within two feet to the left of the plane tree on this side before going to the end of street and then back again to the main road where there, too, he has a mathematically precise itinerary. Sometimes he smiles though never at anyone, only to himself, and I think that smile may be the expression of an accomplishment, maybe a beautifully exercised turn. I have never, in the several years I've observed him up close, been able to catch his eye. I suspect he is a genius of some kind. The other walker is an elderly man, well into his eighties, who is always in suit and tie and sometimes with a small sou'wester that is as much a protection against the sun as against rain. If I were a painter and I could get him to stay put for long enough, which I doubt is possible, I'd paint him, for he has the face of a holy fool such as one finds in certain renaissance paintings. At great speed he covers a territory whose compass is several miles greater than that of the man in the tuque. I have encountered him in two neighbouring boroughs, stooped, in huge concentration, his arms moving as if operating two invisible gears, one forward, one back, paddling the air to either side of him. Would that I could see what these two men see. They are travellers of a kind and I like to think they make some extraordinary discoveries. What would their travelogues be like? I write this in the certain knowledge that somewhere out there, at this very moment, 10:52 a.m., on 16 December 2014, they are on their fabulous trajectories. There are people who travel the world over and never let in a thing or very little, whereas, if I may hazard a guess, the bearded man in the tuque, who never veers from his chosen path, and the man with the Brueghelesque face are two of the great explorers of our age.

ONE TENDS TO SEE things more acutely when somewhere else, and maybe it's because we preserve in ourselves something primitive that watches for woolly mammoths bursting through the foliage. Okay, then, I'll describe one place I've been to. Actually I've been there quite a few times but my aim here is to reduce the many to one. I must seek out, and isolate, the particular. I was in Oxford not long ago and, for once, I kept notes. I went there in order to attend a lecture by Sir Geoffrey Hill, and, thinking I may as well make a day of it, I took an early bus and arrived there in time for a spot of lunch. At the Grand Café on High Street, reputed to be the first coffeehouse in England, a woman in her late thirties, in a patterned beret, sat at the table next to mine. She ordered a bowl of porridge. What sort of woman, I wondered, orders porridge at one in the afternoon. A classics professor? Someone with a complicated personal life? *Who was she?* She had a story, I'm sure. Her cheeks were dabbed with rouge, overly so, a bit like the wooden ballerina in *Coppelia*, and she wore bright red lipstick, a fur coat, blue jeans, and shoes with white spats. No single article of her clothing matched another, which made for a kind of unity. She ate, she paid, she went, another of the world's unsolvable mysteries. I was certain of one thing only: she knew I was writing about her as surely as if I were sketching her from up close. She didn't flinch, nor did she silently yield to my brown study. She'll know herself if ever she reads this.

With time to spare I went to the Ashmolean Museum, settling for a while on its collection of Cycladic figurines, and was not a little dismayed to learn that originally their faces were painted in reds and blues. Suddenly those beautiful white shapes had lost something for me. Ancients with a taste for the gaudy, to hell with them. It had been bad enough seeing earlier a reproduction of a statue of a Roman emperor with the colours in which the original marble would have been painted. What an eyesore. And to think they were all like that, statue upon statue, no wonder the Visigoths sacked Rome. I then wandered into the museum café where I ordered the cream tea. It was not that I so badly wanted one, but whilst away one tends to do the things one would not normally do at home. This was my plan: I'd splurge on a cream tea and then go and hear contemporary literature's *crème de la crème* who, when he is not being overly abstruse, and when he is in Long John Silver mode, is very funny indeed, even touchingly so, such as when he sang the whole of "Sally in our Alley", and when he is not and is deeply sombre, he is the most rigorously intelligent of men, so chock full of knowledge one wonders how he keeps it all in his noddle. Sometimes, when I get the drift of what he is talking about, I come away a speck wiser but often I leave feeling stupider. Who *was* that Elizabethan divine? What *were* those lines from *Piers Plowman*, which he quoted in an antique tongue? A modern rendering is not for the likes of our literary knight and for this he has, if not my comprehension, my praise. I am three times the age of many of the students he addresses and by virtue of my years alone I've read a great deal more than they have, but why is it they smile knowingly and bob their heads at things wholly obscure to me? They are barely out of their cradles. The agonisingly recondite, it's what one gets with the Oxford Professor of Poetry, take it or leave it, and the glory of it all is that he doesn't much care because for him *difficult* is the province of the democratic whereas *easy* is the tool of the fascistic. I'm still mulling that over, and probably I am simplifying things a little, but I appreciate the argument all the same. Maybe today things would be clearer. With this in mind I plunged my knife into the clotted cream, but it was unnaturally solid, not at all like Cornish cream which is of a thickness dictated by nature—this might have been aided by some chemical agency, a thickener such as polyurethane or some high-performance adhesive. It stuck to the knife, all of it, a fatty lump of disquietude. It was a struggle getting some of it back into the dish. I pressed the remainder to the scone which, because it was stale or maybe just improperly baked, collapsed in a pyramid of crumbs. The cream clung to the blade and the jam was still in its small jar and with nothing now that I could spread it over. At one point I even tried to marshal the crumbs into a corral, thinking maybe it could be scooped up and, without too many people noticing, aimed at my mouth in a single upward heave, but they disintegrated even more, from crumb to particle. This battle lost, my heart in a sling, I poured the tea. I was to suffer an even worse shock. It was not the Earl Grey I'd ordered but a ghastly herbal concoction, chamomile, which is said by the wise to steady the nerves. I'd sooner drink a boiled haystack. I was by this point too weary with life to make a scene, and, besides, the girl who served me was Polish and perhaps not a fully accomplished Anglophone although most Poles are. Poles are born linguists and most people are, of course, Polish. I was not about to lash my tongue at fifty per cent of my heritage. I left the crumbs, the untouched jam, and what may have been a cream substitute. And I left behind the pot of herbal piss and the full teacup that accompanied it. The table was a disaster zone. I got to the lecture hall only to discover I was a week early. Why didn't I double-check the date? What was it that allowed me to think it wasn't a week hence? I made my way back to London where, at the outskirts, the bus got caught in a traffic jam. It sat for a full hour and not even the memory of an Oxbridge Coppelia could induce further wonderment in me.

So there's one journey I've made.

I now feel sufficiently emboldened to describe another. It is perfectly feasible in this city of cities to go on a world journey. Some weeks ago, I went to Eritrea, the whole country brought to bear in a small café on the Goldhawk Road near Shepherds Bush Market. It is a fifteen-minute walk from here. The place might have been airlifted whole from Asmara, together with the Formica-topped tables, the hanging lanterns and the clientele who, apart from me, were all Eritrean, most of them refugees, some of them, perhaps, the sons of refugees. One of the former was a middle-aged man in a western business suit, with tribal scars on his face. It is one of the few places where I feel perfectly at ease. London has become so commercially minded there are not many cafés left where one is not made to feel uncomfortable if one lingers over an empty cup. Rumination is not allowable in many places, and the measures are there to prevent it. The equation that time equals money is one of the things that has signalled the death of civilisation, TV screens in restaurants being another. I ordered the coffee. Actually what one orders is a pared down version of the Ethiopian coffee ceremony. There is no young woman in a white cotton dress colourfully embroidered at the edges to serve the coffee. And a ceremony is not easily achieved with just two people or when one is on one's own. It is not, however, a bad simulacrum of the real thing. Also it is absurdly inexpensive. How many cups of coffee need to be consumed to pay the rent for this cavern of a place? The green coffee beans are roasted, crushed, and then put into a beautifully shaped clay vessel called a *jebena* whose spout is stuffed with horse hair which acts as a filter. It is imbibed from small cups called *finjals*. The coffee which is laced with ginger and various spices is so powerful it always shocks at first. Sugar is essential even for people who do not take sugar. It is served with burning frankincense so that any evil spirits might be dispelled in advance of drinking the coffee the consumption of which is said to transform, in three stages, the human spirit. This is why it is properly served in three rounds called *abol*, *tona* and *baraka* with the third being a blessing upon those who partake of this spiritually, and saporifically, most potent brew. It sets one abuzz for hours at a time. Sleeps not he who drinks it after the cock crows. I spoke to the man with scars on his face, who took part in the Eritrean War for Independence. The first question he asked me was whether I enjoyed the coffee. The more one drinks of it, I said, the better it becomes. Someday soon, he replied, he'd invite me to a performance of his country's music and poetry. The other day, wanting a fix, I headed back to the café but it was gone, another casualty of a city where time is money, money time.

A REVIEWER WRITING of the paperback edition of my book, *The Street Philosopher and the Holy Fool*, described my observations with respect to the 'Oriental mind' (did I really employ such a phrase? yes, I believe I did) as being 'curiously outdated'. She was absolutely right because between the publication of the hardback and the soft editions of my book Syria had changed, so dramatically I began to wonder if the criticism with which she dampened her kinder words did not render my book obsolete. When I began work on my next book, *The Pigeon Wars of Damascus* (Biblioasis, 2010), it was with different eyes. But now even that book is outdated. It was largely written during the second Gulf War and *before* the very short Arab Spring during which time hope was reduced to despair in a matter of weeks. Admittedly I did not guess at what would happen in Syria although the book itself guessed at it. Almost unthinkingly I concluded it with the image of a missile landing on a busy marketplace. It had not occurred to me that it might be a Syrian missile. Oddly this failure in sagacity fills me with shame. I feel I ought to have seen what was coming but, and maybe this is a consolation, albeit a weak one, neither did my Syrian friends. What I can say is that the book is one of dark shadows and menace.

A book may be accurate in its details until there comes a stage when it is no longer so, when it becomes 'curiously outdated', and then it enters a kind of cold storage but with luck there may be a third, posthumous kind of existence, when it becomes a record of a time forever lost. Whatever one writes, *whenever* one writes, it is always on the cusp of disappearance.

A photographer told me once that he keeps all his images, even those which he considers failures, because the day will come when even the latter are invested with fresh meaning. One writes to preserve *what's there*. So yes, to set down what one sees, this is one of the purposes of writing, to be able to say, as Goya wrote in the corner of one of his drawings, *yo lo vi* ('I saw it'). There spoke one who might well have seen the nerves behind a flayed man's face.

Christmas, with Kafka

Although Prague at most appears in occasional paraphrases
in Kafka's work, it nevertheless exists everywhere in his writing, like the salt in the water of the Buddhist parables.

–Johannes Urzidil, *There Goes Kafka*

IN THE OLD TOWN SQUARE (Staroměstské náměstí) in
Prague, beneath an enormous Christmas tree, a small manger held live animals of various species. Suddenly there was
a terrible commotion and much cheering from onlookers as
two of its occupants, a donkey and a llama, got into battle. The
llama screamed as the donkey made for its neck and the smaller
creatures, a goat and a lamb and I can't remember what else, fled
the plunging of hooves. The donkey and the llama, their teeth
bared, spun in circles and such was the centrifugal force they
produced that the slatted fence confining them began danger-
ously to bulge. Old farm boy that I am, I shouted and waved
my arms, trying fruitlessly to separate them. There was more
laughter from the mocking circle that put me in mind of the
lumpish figures in Brueghel's *Christ Falling Beneath the Cross*,
whose fleetingly warped faces were painted for all time.

A woman in furs strutted over from the other side of the
square.

'*Basta!*' she said, in a firm voice.

Obediently the animals stopped and the crowd dispersed, doubtless disappointed at so happy an outcome. The creatures brayed a little more and then slunk back into their earlier supporting roles. The wonder is not only that a llama should have been in Bethlehem in the first place, but also that it, as well as the donkey, understood Italian. Who was this lady in furs that she could make a magical wand of her voice? Why had I, in this symbolic Bethlehem, singularly failed to impress with mine? The geographical Bethlehem was, just then, also in a state of warfare. The Israeli Defence Force had recently entered the town and, after declaring it a 'closed military area', imposed a curfew. Palestinian shells were fired from the nearby village of Beit Jala. The hotels were closed, the streets empty, and at the Church of the Nativity a couple of small windows had been broken by Israeli gunfire, apparently the first damage to the church since the Crusades. *Basta, basta.* The papal pleas for calm went unheeded. Christendom, meanwhile, didn't much seem to care. Christendom was on holiday. Christendom pleaded a migraine.

I went to Prague with the dubious notion that I might follow 'the Kafka trail', even though I am an agnostic when it comes to literary pilgrimages. There are maps, guides and tours devoted to such a scheme. If one pays the ludicrous admission to the Zlatá ulička, the 'Golden Lane', which I did not, ghosting my way past the ticket collector instead, one may visit the small dwelling where, in the shadow of Prague Castle, as much as one might have liked it to be the case, Kafka did *not* write *The Castle*. What he wrote instead were some of the stories that were later collected in *A Country Doctor*. A prophetic mind makes small allowance for the trite: the whole street, once home to alchemists and the stuff of life that produces great literature, has been turned into a row of souvenir shops, an idiot's parade. It was not so when I first visited it in 1974, in what were still the grey days of Communism, where, at Zlatá ulička 22, I had to push aside a rack of postcards to discover a plaque commemorating the fact of Kafka's brief domicile there. This, at least, given the politics of the time, was properly Kafkaesque. Now one may purchase a Kafka mug or a T-shirt. Did I see any of his books for sale? Pity the memory of any writer whose image appears on a plate or on the handle of a spoon. One may easily guess how Kafka would have reeled at the industry spawned in his name.

It is easier, in some respects, for a city to recover from the fuselage of war than from the puffballs of peace. True enough, Prague has been restored to its former beauty but only to be adorned with cheap trinkets. The moves to accommodate tourism are probably more irreversible there than just about anywhere else I have been to, which is not to say that by means of some benign force the tourist shops could not be closed, sledgehammers taken to the hideous glass objects on sale, and, as punishment for so much of Prague's atrocious cuisine, the heads of a hundred cooks impaled on the Charles Bridge. Almost immediately I abandoned 'the Kafka trail', realising, as I ought to have done earlier, that for any such efforts to be mentally or spiritually rewarding depends not so much upon deliberation as upon how the clouds move. Actually, without having yet realised it, I had already experienced something not to be found in any tourist guide. The incident in the manger might well have come from Kafka's own pen. Surely he would not have been indifferent to such a scene. After all, he was born, had lived and gone to school in this very square. 'My whole life,' Kafka wrote to his Hebrew teacher, Friedrich Thieberger, 'is confined to this small circle.'

When may a square be rightly called a circle?

I have spoken of my agnosticism in the matter of literary pilgrimages. What is it that one expects to find when one goes to the house where a writer lived or when one visits his grave? The bed where he slept is, more often than not, not his but another bed altogether, a bed in the style of what *might* have been his, and, often enough, the wood of which it is made is the wood that enters the expectant features of one's face. And *still* one strikes a foolishly thoughtful pose. And the tomb beneath which our hero lies is, after all, not something he ever lived to see. What, then, by visiting them, cradle and grave, do we hope to reconstruct for ourselves? Sometimes, though, something happens and it is not quite what one anticipates.[1] One enters a zone, so to speak, where the direction one takes is not a physical one. There can be no purchasing a ticket to that place. The ancient Greeks might speak here of *epiphaneia* which, before the Christians made the word uniquely theirs, meant 'appearance' but which also carried with it the idea of divine intervention or manifestation. Maybe, though, it is simply a matter of having the gods on one's side.

WE WENT THE FOLLOWING evening to a performance of Janáček's opera *The Cunning Little Vixen*. I have not been able to discover any connection between the composer and Kafka and sadly I must conclude they were not aware of each other's existence,[2] nor have I been able to find any mention in Kafka's

---

1   When I visited Keats's grave, in February 1974, it was with a bag of blood oranges. It was the act of peeling one beside his anonymous tombstone, not something that I'd planned to do, which I did only because I wanted refreshment, that later led to my writing a poem called "The Blood Oranges." Although of no great literary value, it stands with my more honourable failures: the poem bespoke—and it must have been, I believe, that bright red drop appearing at the surface of the inner skin that inspired me—a transfusion of some kind, not between the living and the dead as such but rather between myself and some idea floating in me, which would not have been the case were it not for the blood orange and which would have had no significance had I not consumed it beside Keats's grave.

2   I stand corrected, twice: in a letter to *PN Review*, where this piece first appeared, Graham Roe writes: 'Perhaps I am being obtuse, but surely Max Brod is the connection. In literary circles Brod, although himself a novelist, is known as the editor and biographer of Kafka. In musical circles Brod, although himself a composer, is known

diaries and letters of a marvellous painter, hitherto unknown to me, whose canvases I saw that morning for the first time. Surely Kafka, had he known about the Czech Symbolist, Jan Preisler (1872–1918), would have made mention of him. Preisler owes much, it is true, to Puvis de Chavannes, but he is his own distinct voice. He produced only a handful of paintings and then, apparently unable to come to grips with what he believed was the threat to his vision posed by Picasso, Kandinsky and Braque, he succumbed to depression and painted no more. I admire in particular his haunting 'Black Lake' series, which in their foregrounds depict a naked youth together with a white horse, paintings that are deeply suggestive and at the same time, as in those of Piero della Francesca, radiantly immobile.

---

as one of the first critics to recognise Janáček's genius and as the German translator of several of Janáček's operas, which first became known outside Czechoslovakia in his versions. The friendships overlapped between 1916, when Brod and Janáček met, and 1924, when Kafka died. It is possible, I suppose, that Brod never mentioned one to the other, but this seems unlikely. Two very likely occasions for a mention can be found quickly in Ernst Pawel's *The Nightmare of Reason: A Life of Franz Kafka*. The first was in March 1918, when Bruno Kafka, a cousin of Franz, who was a right-wing politician, protested to the authorities about a performance of Janáček's *Jenufa* in Prague on the grounds that it compromised the "German character" of the city: this despite the fact that the performance was given using Brod's translation of the libretto into German. The second was in March 1924, when Brod went to Berlin for the première there of *Jenufa* and met Kafka … Brod says in his biography that Kafka was not at all musical, so perhaps Kafka would have taken no notice of a mention of Janáček. However, Janáček was certainly interested in literature, and would surely have been intrigued to hear Kafka. I hope that some real scholar can provide more definite facts.' In the following issue of *PNR*, Kafka's most recent biographer, Nicholas Murray, writes: 'Graham Roe pleads for "a real scholar" to step forward to say whether Kafka and Janáček were aware of each other's existence. It really only needs someone to consult the index to his correspondence where there are many references to the composer in letters to Brod. A representative one would be in October 1917 when Kafka thanks Brod for sending him his translation of *Jenufa*, remarking it will serve "as tomorrow's treat in my reclining chair" (*Letters to Friends, Family and Editors* (1978), translated by Richard and Clara Winston, p. 151). There is no apparent evidence that the composer and the writer met but the latter was certainly aware of the existence of the former.'

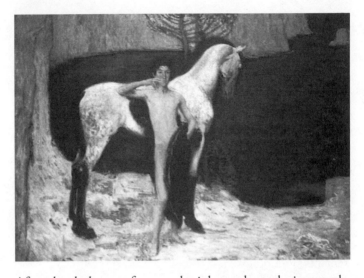

After the drabness of so much eighteenth- and nineteenth-century Czech painting—I do not apologise for my feelings of tedium—Preisler's paintings were like a sudden burst of light heralding the even brighter flash that would soon illumine the whole of Prague, what was to be a revolution in art, music, literature and architecture equal, in sheer vitality, to what was going on in Paris and elsewhere at the time. Only in Prague has Art Deco impressed me, coming, as it does, as natural heir to the Czech Baroque. As for the music I can only imagine it is a sublime response to the stodgy cuisine. It was the Janáček opera that would provide me with the next of my Kafkaesque epiphanies. Although the production of the *Vixen* had not won the approval of the Czech critics who grumble at even the slightest change to their beloved composer's schema there was something in it that fully brought home to me just how incredibly strange that opera is. I had previously thought it overly cute, just a bit too folksy for its own good, but how wrong I was. After the vixen's death three-quarters of the way through, when the plot has nowhere to go, we begin to observe the workings of human nature from another angle, as it were, and in what is surely one of the strangest aftermaths in all opera the audience itself takes on a posthumous role. The snippets of the human comedy on stage are observed as if from our, or, rather, the dead vixen's, eyes. The sense of dislocation in which suddenly we find ourselves is reminiscent of something else, namely Gregor Samsa's awakening into a new and terrifying perspective on ordinary human existence. 'Whoever partakes of the fox's tongue,' goes a line in the opera's libretto, 'becomes invisible.'

THE CAFÉ LOUVRE on Národní třída is where Kafka and Max Brod went as part of a philosophic circle devoted to the writings of Franz Brentano, but it was more for itself than for its literary associations that I went there several times. The food was bearable, there was no pop music, and the place hummed of *ancien régime*. The café had been painted over in bureaucratic green, chopped up and turned into offices during the Communist regime but was now restored to its former dusty pink state. Those commissars feared more than anything beauty and grace. Slaughter both and the world's yours to do with as you like. A woman at the table opposite gazed absent-mindedly through her own blown cloud of smoke. A salvo of billiard balls echoed from the room beyond, and a waiter zipped back and forth, perfectly schooled in the art of avoidance. The walls were hung with photographic nudes. All was quickly obliterated by some rather unseemly behaviour in the turtle tank where—whether for pleasure or from sheer boredom—two of its several occupants were taking a libidinous route. At another of Kafka's favourite haunts, the Montmartre, instead of the cabaret music he listened to, heavy metal crushed the silences. A boorish youth openly and at length squeezed his girlfriend's left breast. They seemed as unfathomable as the turtles.

I stood at Kafka's grave in Židovské hřbitovy cemetery—a blustery day, the sun breaking through the clouds now and then, and with not a tourist in sight, a rare and sweet solitude. All would have been spoiled otherwise. I knew, and the fear of it quickened my every step, that whole busloads of people came here. The Kafka family tombstone, designed by the architect Leopold Ehrmann, is lovelier than any photograph can demonstrate because its Cubist design makes such demands on the space surrounding it and, in return, is defined by that space. Ivan Margolius, author of *Prague: A guide to twentieth-century architecture* (Artemis, 1994) writes:

> In 1911 the architect Pavel Janák identified two form-making forces in nature: the horizontal level of water and the vertical direction of weight. Other more complicated forms were created by a third diagonal force, a power resident within matter. The best example of this power is in crystallization. The force concentrated within the crystals is so strong that it overcomes weight. If vertical and horizontal planes are the forms of calmness and balance of matter, diagonally shaped forms are created by more dramatic action and the complicated union of forces. By the inclusion of the third, diagonal plane one can implant soul into matter and convey dramatic action. There was no better way to symbolize Kafka's complex personality, which gave the world his far-reaching literary achievement than by using a crystal form and all the energy and mystery it encapsulated.

I am not sure if I fully grasp his meaning but it was there, at Kafka's grave, that Margolius made a striking discovery. On the other side of the tombstone, buried head to head, as it were, was the grave of his great-grandfather who also died in 1924.

I wanted to leave a stone at Kafka's grave. The tombstone, because of its crystalline shape, would not allow for the placing of a stone anywhere on its surface and so I knelt down to add it to the small pyramid of stones that was already there. And then it struck me that the addition of my stone might bring all the others tumbling down. I would have to reassemble the pile and this, I feared, would be close to impossible. The stones had been set there with infinite care, one by one, over who knows what period of time. Already I had a vision of them rolling all over the place or perhaps, yes, perhaps just one would begin to slide and as I sought to arrest it another two would be dislodged and then, as I pursued those, progressively more. I found myself locked into what the poet Christopher Middleton, when I told him the story, would describe as 'a perfect instance of Kafkaesque aboulia'. Later, I discovered that Irena Murray (née Žantovská), the lady at whose flat I stayed in Prague, had written a tale based on her own experience, in which she describes a similar predicament, only in her case it was not a stone but a chestnut, which would have been

27

even more difficult to keep in place. She had been unable to find a stone. I had difficulty finding one. At last, however, I managed ever so delicately to place my stone without causing the much-dreaded avalanche but when I left, with a stinging in my eyes, it was with the absolute certainty that no one else would be able to add another one.

A Winter in Gabes

A SEMI-WILD DOG, BARED FANG and flying saliva, stands at the beginning of this prose. This snarling creature, so tightly wound up it could despatch me at a single bite, is, I believe, the one we encountered in the oasis at Gabes. It blocked our path with such ferocity there was nothing else for us to do but abandon our search for windfall pomegranates, which had been left to rot in their hundreds, and to turn back home. 'Stop,' it seems to be saying to me, 'how will you manage to convince anyone of these stale memories?' These are, I realise, awfully foolish words to put into the mouth of a dog whose preferred taste is not for ideas but for human flesh. I do wonder, however, at the wisdom of writing at a remove of over three decades, when so much seems already to have vanished into a haze. Where will be the intelligence such as only fresh images projected against a blank screen provide? Still, and not only because I've been invited to, I will attempt now to slink past the snarling creature my doubts recreate.

We went to Tunisia in the winter of 1973 with a view to my finding an inexpensive place in which to live and write. Such was the thinking then, especially among young literary tyros, that one could create only in Mediterranean climes. One needed the right clothes, of course, the right girl at one's side. One could drink only the roughest wine. Aim too high and one's credentials were in tatters. North Africa had never been in our thoughts as a possible destination and, after our failure to find a place on the Greek island of Santorini, our decision to go there was admittedly a somewhat random one. We booked a flight from Athens, via Rome, to Tunis. After a few days in Tunis, of which I remember little, we went to Hammamet with its lovely painted blues. We had nothing but trouble there, however, and late one night had to flee the house where our host insisted that it was the custom of the country that he be allowed to sleep with the lady a male guest brings with him. When I protested at my having to defer to traditional values he gave a whistle and immediately the room filled up with his friends. God knows what their understanding of the situation was, but we were not in the best position from which to argue. We calmly packed our bags as we spoke, made our escape, and that night took shelter in the shell of a house under construction, listening to the dogs barking in the distance. We had other such mishaps but to catalogue them would be to produce a not wholly sympathetic picture of a people who were otherwise warm and hospitable.

We blundered our way south to the coastal town of Gabes. There we found a cheap place, the Hôtel de la Gare, managed by a gaunt man in a fez and a toothbrush moustache. Monsieur le Patron, as we called him, not a little ironically, hardly ever moved from his position by the door. What small amounts of food he ate were brought to him along with a daily supply of cigarettes. Awake, not awake; upright, prone—these were his principal modes of existence. Whatever his limitations, or perhaps because of them, he was quite beyond the reach of surprise. When, for our Christmas decoration, we brought home an armload of branches pulled from a pine tree, probably the only pine tree in Gabes, not even then did he express curiosity. All he ever did was *be*. After three months, we never even got to know his name. The hotel was by no means the cleanest or the niftiest of places and when, at first, we remonstrated, with a view to his lowering the weekly rates, he replied, in what was the longest conversation we would ever have, '*Monsieur, c'est un hôtel propre.*' There was something wearily noble in his response. We began with a room in the middle of the building, which had no windows and, soon after, moved to one with a window looking out onto the street. The view comprised a concrete shed, a road continually under repair, an electrical line, and two palm trees.

A few *dinars* more and we could have stayed at the hotel down the street that served briefly during World War Two as General Rommel's headquarters. (There was a sheltered dune not far away where it was claimed one could still see the German tank tracks. I wonder, though, if they were not nightly applied.) We were on a tight budget, however, and besides, what we would have missed had we not stayed at the Hôtel de la Gare. A window on the world is a cliché, of course, but that's what it became. A boy cleaned our room weekly although we had to plead with him not to—the tattered cloth at the end of his stick only served to spread the filth still further across our floor. Such housework as had to be done we did ourselves. We did most of our cooking there, over a single flame, becoming ever more inventive, and slowly, slowly we eroded our minds with rough Tunisian wine. The music from the downstairs café would have been fine, a scratchy record of Om Khalthoum, but for the fact it was the only record they owned and this, played over and over, especially when I was violently sick for a week, did little to calm the nerves.

While I ought to have been recording my impressions of Gabes all my energies went into the writing of a surrealist novel, the only draft of which I left there, in that room, in a dustbin. It may still be there. I remember nothing of the book other than there was one passage the composition of which moved me to tears. Whatever it was, it must have been truly

dire. The impressions of Tunisia I took away were more powerful and memorable than anything I wrote. The shame of it is
that an entire book could have come of my experiences there.
Quite honestly, I didn't know there was a genre called travel
literature, although the fact of my not knowing might have
been a boon. I might have written something even worse, a
book of 'travellers' tales'. Sadly, though, given the people I met
and the things I saw, I took away not so much as a scribbled
note.

We were fortunate enough to have visited Tunisia before
it became a major holiday destination although I suspect
that even in our relative innocence we were part of what had
begun to effect a decline. We knew not enough to be wise,
or so says the slavering dog at my ankle. At least we never
allowed ourselves to be immunised against experience. We
moved among the people and they got to know us. A human
slick has polluted the world's shores and it has seeped inland
sucking into itself the very life from villages, towns and even
cities. The few tourists we saw stayed mostly at expensive
beach hotels, those immaculate garrisons of the mediocre, or
else were seen descending from air-conditioned buses, after
which they would walk about the *souq* for ten minutes before
being whisked away to the next destination. They were, some
of them, quite the most repulsive people I had ever seen. I
remember in particular two obese men in tight white shorts,
one of whom was having his shoes polished by a street urchin
while the other filmed them. The fat men laughed and the
little Arab boy smiled the sickening smile that came of hoping
for a few extra *dinars*. The more remote places were as yet
undefiled. I was fortunate enough to stay in the desert town of
Nefta. The last I heard of it there is now a desert resort at the
edge of the Sahara, a five-star hotel where the tourists drink
martinis beside a swimming pool that uses up most of the
town's supply of water and then they 'experience' the desert

in dune buggies. Another shock was seeing a woman in a red bikini walk through the Berber village of Matmata. She must have felt the people there were too inconsequential for it to matter whether or not the greater part of her body was visible to them. There were already the beginnings of sex tourism and among many young men in the coastal towns there was an uneasy mixture of apathy and oily corruption. They would spend hours in the cafés, playing their mindless games, one of which involved flicking a small matchbox from the edge of the table, trying to land it on one of its six sides, five points for the long, ten for the short sides. Only the older men played chess or backgammon, games that required intelligence.

There was never any sense these young people would be able to move on in life—massive unemployment and sheer boredom (this last surely the most pernicious of social diseases) slackened them both physically and mentally. The only break in the pattern was when they found themselves on the make. We were much too annoyed by them to feel the compassion one may now feel at a greater distance. Any Western woman was for them indistinguishable from the images presented in a score of dreadful imported movies or magazines although, in truth, there were women, mostly from northern Europe, who came to places like Djerba looking for sexual experience. The strapping boys they came for were the same boys the men, also mostly from northern Europe, combed the beaches for. There can be no calculating the spiritual and moral devastation wrought by these Nordic invaders and what we witnessed was only the beginning of something that was to grow over the years. When, later, I went inland and met Tunisians as yet untouched by tourism, they would shake their heads sadly at the fates of their coastal brethren.

Gabes was a town of few antiquities and not much more by way of pretty scenes and was therefore not interesting enough to be overly corrupted by tourism. We made our home there with greater ease than we would have, say, in Hammamet or even Sfax. The superb beaches were relatively bare. There was one major hotel just outside town but only rarely did we glimpse the people staying there. And so, without the continual pressures of being taken for potential buyers of fake antiquities, we found Gabes a good place in which to settle. Also, it was also a useful base from which to take short trips into country. I will skate over my meetings with Arabs in the interior, when I ventured there on my own, for there is nothing in such an account that many other people will not have experienced in varying degrees—the incredible hospitality, the friendly talk, the biblical offerings of milk and dates. As wonderful as those experiences might have been to an initiate—which, after all, is what I was—their value as narrative stays mainly on the surface. I would like, however, to mention Ahmad ben Amara, the young man who invited me to stay with his family in the old village of Kebili and whose kindness and moral seriousness set forever the seal on my deep affection for the Arab people. I was allowed to wear his father's traditional robes; I ate from the same bowl with them; I danced at a wedding party with men my own age; we slept on the same floor; we swore undying allegiances.

(Ahmad holds the camera, probably the first time he has ever held one. I blush at the younger me so self-conscious in his pyjama'd father's robes.)

All this was heady stuff for a man in his early twenties. I sought to repay Ahmad in kind by inviting him back to Gabes. I was much too callow to realise the deep discomfort he would feel upon having to socialise with me in the presence of a strange woman and even my cooking a meal in both his and her presence was too much for him to take. Ahmad had probably never been anywhere further than Gabes. The worst was to come when I invited him, innocently enough, to share our quarters, which comprised only a single room. I did not realise so much could be so quickly undone. Almost immediately Ahmad returned home, pleading some lame excuse, the promise of his own mattress not being sufficient to keep him there. I hope he remembers me, who knew not enough to be wise, with something other than feelings of acute dismay.

Once we had established ourselves in Gabes and had become familiar figures in the *souq* and in one or two cafés, we could go everywhere, unmolested and unpursued. If the people we got to know best in Gabes were mostly foreigners living there I would have to argue that they formed an integral part of our travel experiences. One could still meet people such as one encounters in the novels of Graham Greene—the British consul, seemingly forgotten, metaphorically covered with cobwebs, the French who were so insular they spoke only to each other, and the young Americans, many of them attached to the Peace Corps, and some of whom had a disturbing brightness in their eyes.

Among the latter was a singular person of missionary zeal, Fritz, a thin, humourless man with a disagreeable blonde bristle for a moustache, who kept a distance from his fellow Americans and probably from most of the human race.

A loner he may have been, set in his ways certainly, but he had taken the trouble to learn Arabic. This was impressive although whenever he spoke it, his listeners, sadly for him, betrayed little or no surprise. I fell in with Fritz for a while; perhaps I even liked him, as has always been my tendency with people furthest removed from the centre of commonsensical society. Fritz, though, was not a man one could love. There could be no pulling him away from the straight line of his life, whatever that was, no cracking of a joke at his expense. Fritz was, in spirit, as serious as a brand new toothbrush, ready to apply himself with vigour to the world's unclean surfaces. I joined Fritz on a short journey to the Berber village of Matmata, in the south of the country, where apparently he had some business.

Matmata has been vividly described elsewhere, *too* vividly, perhaps, for it has become now a major tourist site. A way of life has been forever ruined. The Berbers of old had devised for themselves an ingenious form of dwelling, a system of underground rooms joined by connecting tunnels, at the centre of which was a sunken courtyard. When seen from above, these dwellings, grouped together, made for a kind of lunar landscape. It was, in short, not a town over which one would wish to run at great speed on a starless night. It was here that the unbending line of Fritz's life touched upon a foreign circumference. While staring down into one of subterranean dwellings he had his great vision: he would make it his mission to introduce the battery hen to the Berbers of Matmata. After getting one of the families to agree to the experiment he had the chickens brought in at his own expense. At the bottom of the crater, in their readymade coop, the chickens enjoyed their first and last breakfast. A few hours later, beneath the noonday sun, they were baked alive. When I went with Fritz to Matmata he discussed with the Berbers, in Arabic, emendations to his earlier plan but they seemed not at all interested in his hare-brained schemes. Clearly, he was to be avoided and, besides, they preferred their birds stringy and tough; a plump, juicy chicken was anathema to them. Moreover, they plucked the hens while still alive so as to tense up the muscles in their bodies. It was as clear an illustration of misplaced altruism as any I had ever seen. I wonder in what corridor of power, imagined or otherwise, Fritz the Chicken Man now plans his next move.

THE MOST FASCINATING FIGURE of all was a Hungarian in his early fifties, with piercing eyes and a goatee, who wore a threadbare sports jacket, dirty canvas trousers and a turban and who limped about town with a bundle of old newspapers. Why didn't I make a note of his name? He had been living in Gabes for many years, certainly long enough for him to know all the ropes. Unstintingly, he would offer us his advice. 'Yes, you may eat here but not in that restaurant over there. When the German Army came the officers ate there and the present owner's father served them. You must avoid the place.' I wish I had discovered why it was he lived in Gabes, but in our conversations with him, although he would swing between familiarity and distance, we were always aware of but could never quite gauge a secret life. He was, so he claimed, the rightful heir to the Hungarian throne and while this may not have been strictly true he was, in his polished gestures, in the clipped manner of his speech and in the way he smoked his cigarette on an ivory holder, a man of certain pedigree. What I did not realise at the time was that his life had already indirectly crossed mine.

One day, untying the string that held his newspapers together, he asked me whether it wasn't terrible, the news from London. He took from the top of the pile a yellowing copy of the *Daily Mirror,* dating from 1952, which related the story of a Polish countess who had been murdered in

a small hotel in Earls Court. As I stared at the old head-
lines it occurred to me that I knew something about this
woman and her miserable death. It was only recently when
trying to identify her so that I might in turn provide a fac-
tual basis to my story of the Hungarian that I began on
my researches. She turned out to be the famous Special
Operations Executive, Krystyna Skarbek, better known by
her *nom de guerre*, Christine Granville. The man who had
been her husband, Jerzy Giżycki, stayed in the house where
my parents, my uncle and my grandfather lived in 1948,
near the small village of Burritts Rapids in the eastern town-
ships of Ontario. Although he had lived with them for over a
year, paying twenty-five cents room and board a day, he had
made no mention of a wife. It was only a few years later, in
1952, when my mother was sent from England a copy of the
Daily Mirror, the very same issue the Hungarian had with
him in Tunisia, and which mentions Giżycki by name, that
she was able to put together the pieces.[1]

What about the Hungarian? I now ask myself. What was
he doing in a small town in Tunisia, carrying with him, all
those years later, a newspaper relating the story of Christine
Granville's murder? Who was he and why was he there? There
were also questions I could *not* have asked him. What was he
running away from? What had driven him over the edge? I
doubt he is still alive. I have made enquiries, thinking that
somebody somewhere must remember this familiar figure of
the streets, but for now his identity will have to remain a
gaping hole in this story. When it came time for us to leave
Gabes I decided he should have the books I'd brought with
me, Genet's *A Thief's Journal*, Kafka's *The Castle*, Durrell's
The Alexandrian Quartet and Camus' *The Outsider*. I made
enquiries as to the Hungarian's whereabouts and found the

---

1   A fuller account of this story appears in my book *The Pebble Chance* (Biblioasis,
2014), pp.125–130.

hovel where he lived, together with some Tunisian youths who gathered about me, making lewd suggestions, reaching for my privates, and who, quite obviously, comprised some kind of homosexual retinue. The poor Hungarian was not at all pleased that I had discovered his miserable quarters and an aspect of his life hitherto unrevealed to me. He shouted at the youths to go away and accepted my books but only with the greatest diffidence. I, for my part, was deeply sorry to have exposed him.

I COULD HAVE CONFINED these memories to what took place outside our window, on the second floor of the dingy Hôtel de la Gare, for it was from there, only a few feet away from where I scribbled away at a book of no consequence, that we were to witness events of natural, political and tragic dimensions. We observed weddings and funerals, women bearing impossibly sized loads on their heads, children playing their street games. Also, that window opened onto farcical scenes. Although traffic was sparse the authorities saw fit to construct a curious round-about, something like a figure eight, that as far as I could see served no purpose whatsoever. The true nature of its folly, however, was that it was built in such a way that any two cars meeting there were bound to collide. This apparent inability to wed matter and spirit is something I recognise in my own character. One of the more common sights we saw was that of a car motor on a small cart pulled by a mule. Another time we watched in amusement as a man took a hammer to the motor of his car and then, after smashing it several times, jumped away as the car leapt back to life. Other times, too, that window framed the feelings of boredom that are somehow inevitable in the Arab world, which feed the sense that nothing will ever change. We took bets on which of two flies would quit the window or which of two drops of water would fall first. That stillness was illusory, however, for we were soon to witness dramatic changes.

One day there was a hurricane, such as the Mediterranean hurls from time to time against an unsuspecting populace. The two palm trees outside our window bent like bows, the huge arrowheads of their leaves firing in all directions. The road became a virtual river of floating ice. I never did understand from where the ice came. The rain came through the partially open roof of the hotel at such speed that later, when we opened the door to our room, the water rushed in, bringing the flood we saw outside onto the second floor of our building. We were marooned on our bed for a while. We learned later that a busload of children had been swept to their deaths.

The next major event we witnessed from our window was political in nature. President Habib Bourguiba, during one of his not infrequent mental lapses, announced the merger of his country with Libya. Qaddafi was a much-admired figure here in the south of the country, a man who had done much to restore Arab pride and who had brought Libya forward into the twentieth century, particularly with his modernisation of hospital care, a matter of near obsession with him; in short, he was, despite his dubious activities elsewhere, a local hero, another Gamal Abdel Nasser, for Tunisia, it seemed, was about to be pulled from the economic and political doldrums. No sooner was the announcement made than crowds thronged onto the streets, celebrating, the police cheering alongside them. When Bourguiba's wife and son who were away at the time heard the news they rushed home, packed him off to a sanatorium in Geneva, and immediately had his decision reversed. The same people who had been revelling the night before were now protesting and the same police who had walked beside them now donned their riot gear and wielded truncheons. Nicknamed the "American police" because the USA had equipped them, they now set upon the people with ferocity. I tried to photograph the action but the police chased me back into the hotel. I never did hear any reports of deaths or injuries but then there was a complete news blackout; communications were severed between different parts of the country and there were roadblocks everywhere.

On Christmas Eve we heard shots outside. I rushed to the window and there we saw a soldier, a gun in his hand, pursuing an older man. The man tripped and there, partially hidden from view, the soldier emptied his bullets into him. The soldier calmly removed a cigarette from a pack he had tucked in his shirt pocket, lit it, and then unhurriedly walked away without, so it seemed, a care in the world. It was a few minutes before anyone dared move to the scene of the killing. That night, walking through Gabes, I could hear from inside the houses the sound of the *ziraleet*, the ritual crying of the women. There was much occasion for public sorrow for this had been the first murder in living memory.

The story bore all the hallmarks of tragedy, of how in an all too rapidly changing world people act according to the old codes. The soldier had recently married the man's daughter and had given him the dowry, which, in most cases, is a hefty sum. The wife for reasons unknown proved to be unsatisfactory so the soldier divorced her, presumably by clapping his hands thrice, then went to the café downstairs, where the father-in-law was a regular, and demanded that his dowry be returned to him. The father reminded the soldier of a recent change in the law, stipulating that once a dowry had been paid there was no obligation to return it in the event of a failed marriage. The soldier was having none of this, however, and, acting within the expectations of the old code, advised his father-in-law to reconsider the matter otherwise he would be obliged to kill him. The old man was given an hour in which to decide. The soldier returned. The father, realising there was nothing in the new order of things that could protect him, fled the café. And in the old world, where a man's pride is second in importance only to his religious faith, the soldier pursued and killed him with a clear conscience. I asked someone why it was the soldier had so little to fear that he could casually light up a cigarette. I was told that for an action that would have been pardonable only a few months before he would now be sent to the guillotine.

'What else was there for him to do,' my informant added, 'but light up a cigarette?'

WE LEFT TUNISIA SOON AFTER. We took an early morning boat from Tunis to Palermo and at the port, where we spent the night in a waiting room, we had to endure a stoned American hippy asking everyone he came across when the next boat for Malta was. His voice was like a pneumatic drill in the skull, without even the slightest fluctuation of tone. We were glad to be shot of him. A couple of hours later, en route to Palermo, we heard a ghostly voice from somewhere deep inside the vessel, 'Hey, man, is this the boat to Malta?'

A hellhound whines from somewhere even deeper in the ship's hold.

'Moonlight and Vodka'

I HAVE BEEN READING *The Journal of Friar William of Rubruck*, a thirteenth-century account of travels among the Tartars, which is remarkable for its powers of observation or, rather, for the contemporary feel it evokes. The author had an eye unclouded by the religiose and so fresh is his narrative style, so uncluttered his prose, one can just about smell the horse manure. I am particularly grateful for the description of men skimming over ice, on skates fashioned from animal bones and tied to the bottoms of their shoes. One senses here, to employ an already hackneyed phrase, the shock of the new. Also, as if one didn't know already, the book serves to illustrate what a fearsome bunch those Tartars were. The punishments for seemingly mild transgressions, such as approaching a master's chair from the wrong side, were severe while often murder was looked upon with indulgence. It is the minutiae of their lives that especially intrigue me, the fact, for example, that Tartars never went back by the same road they came. It was also considered bad luck to pass by an abandoned encampment where the fires had not fully burned down. I wonder if these strictures might not be applied to the writing of prose.

I started reading the book in Moscow, appropriately enough, where I think I spotted quite a few Tartar faces.

If the manner of my approach is somewhat tangential, the challenge, perhaps, is to make it more so. I had never felt so deprived of the power to communicate. Muscovites, for a start, seem fully locked into themselves. Only rarely does one catch another person's eye, but then, as Mariusz Wilk, in his superb *Journals of a White Sea Wolf*, reminds us, or rather, as Wilk quoting Joseph de Maistre, reminds himself, 'This country is an entirely different world and it is impossible to make any judgement about it without having lived here for some time.' I am speaking of the public face, of course, but I think that to boast an acquaintance with even the private would be to strike against knowledge. I say this, feeling as I do, through its music and literature, a greater intimacy with the mythical Russian psyche than with any other on earth, including that of the mythical Polish one.

On the first day, wandering about Moscow, I found myself in front of the Lubyanka where my father was imprisoned for almost a year. I hadn't meant to go there, not immediately that is. There was something in the very dimensions of that sickly yellowish stone edifice that revolted me, such that I turned and walked away as quickly as possible. I had the sense, too, that the rows of windows were like so many blinded eyes. My father never saw the place from the outside and, given the fact he was confined to a small isolation cell most of the time, he did not see much of it from the inside either. Things happened there of which he never spoke. The Polish poet Aleksander Wat speaks of the Lubyanka as 'a factory that destroys your sense of time.' It robbed my father of his youth with the result, perhaps, that he was unable to comprehend mine. Across the square from the Lubyanka is *Dyetsky Mir*, the largest children's shop in the country.

An eminent psychiatrist told me once that one cannot dream of the dead, which made me wonder what his hourly fees were. That first night in Moscow I dreamed of my father who had died three months before. The dream could not have lasted above a minute. 'How long have you been living in London?' he asked me, with the worried look of one who is mentally trying to recover time. 'Eight years,' I replied, and then, realising my mistake, I corrected myself, saying, 'I mean thirty, almost *thirty* years now,' at which point he vanished. The following day, the dream still clinging to me, I realised it was mathematically true, that in the dream he was in his early sixties, which was the age he was when I had already been living in London for eight years, and that by emending my answer, by entering *real* time, as it were, I had caused him to disappear. Sometimes dreams have their own hidden coordinates. A dream is what it is—the oracular is what we choose it to be.

The next day I walked boldly through the Lubyanka entrance.

A uniformed man inside tried to shoo me away, repeating, 'No museum! No museum!' I signalled to him to calm down and pulled two documents from the brown envelope I had with me, furry-edged, heavily sellotaped, receipts for belongings my father had taken from him at the time of his incarceration, and which he held onto for the rest of his life. My objective now was to reclaim what was rightfully his. I was instructed to go the building opposite. After further shrugs and mumbled officialese, I was finally given an audience with a sympathetic young woman, a child of the *new* Russia, who asked me what I was after. I said I would like to have access to my father's prison files. She told me to write a letter addressed to the director, which she would subsequently translate for me. She then asked me when my father 'disappeared' and when I told her, no, he survived, she looked at me blankly, perhaps wondering why I was wasting her time. I have heard nothing since.

Strangely Moscow was not to be a manufactory of nightmares. I will go so far as to say I rather liked the place. A week later, I would feast upon St. Petersburg's cultural riches, but, for me, Moscow still had the greater edge. I did what most people visiting for the first time do, and so I will dispense with glowing descriptions of museums and churches. There is, however, just one observation I would like to make. I have always wondered about the status of works of religious art that have been removed from churches and put inside museums, whether, by virtue of that transference, they become secularised. We may admire a Piero della Francesca for its formal, and even for its spiritual, qualities, but rarely do we get to breathe the incense. I saw in the Tretyakov Museum something I'd never seen before: a Russian Orthodox priest lay prostrate before Andrei Rublev's *Holy Trinity* and then a man in a business suit did the same, and, still later, much to the annoyance of a security guard, a woman kissed the glass covering the image, leaving there a faint smudge. Church was wherever these images were.

MASHA AVERYNOVA IS, I suspect, the warrior queen of a forgotten tribe. I can easily picture her in a chariot not dissimilar to the huge Pazyryk one made entirely of birch, fourth-century BC, which I saw later in the Hermitage in St. Petersburg. She is not merely tall—she is, in every respect, a giantess. When I first met her, the sun's rays picked up the gold in her teeth, which in ancient times would have been the gold hanging from every part of her. She dresses wholly in black and her hair is black too. She is the widow of my late friend, William Hoffer, whose story is worthy of biographical treatment. The only problem is that no two people would ever agree on his complex nature. Bill was an antiquarian bookseller in Vancouver, a small publisher of poetry and prose, including some of my own, and the Commander-in-Chief of TANKS, a pseudo-military operation he devised in order to rid the world of arts bureaucracies and the collaborators who keep them in place. A fierce opponent of government subsidies, he sought to expose the system of favours that pervade every area of the arts in Canada and elsewhere. I became, during that short but heroic age, District Commissioner for Europe. We sent each other regular communiqués from the battlefield, casualty figures and so forth, dwelling, in particular, on our own dashing manoeuvres. There were, of course, neither tanks nor casualties. We even falsified figures. We pronounced as dead people who were still very much alive. And the Front was wherever we decided it was. I think it's fair to say we were the merrily driven victims of dubious enthusiasm.

POETS, MOSTLY BAD ONES, were the chief targets of Bill's ire. One could build an argument for poetry being, in his mind, the purest of art forms and therefore the most corruptible, but I suspect the main thrust of his campaign against poets had its roots in his inability to ever be one himself. As publisher, he followed his fancies. As bookseller, he had a witch-finder's nose. As critic, he swung between the erratic and the precise. When he hit, he hit hard. Pity the poet whose intellect he described as being akin to a very thin layer of ice covering a huge lake. And then there was the suppressed one-line obituary notice in which he wrote that although he had been saddened to hear of the manner by which a certain poet was silenced, he was grateful for the silence nonetheless. Another poet he described as 'walking about like some Greek god nobody has ever heard of.' Bill Hoffer was not a man to be allowed airtime. The support he gave to several poets was, perhaps, a resolving of an inner conflict but in this, as in everything else, he pushed too far.

Argument, he claimed, was a poor substitute for action. 'I don't want your ideas about literature,' he cried. 'I want body counts!' The day would come when 'war criminals,' as he described his foes, would crawl towards, and willingly immolate themselves upon, heaps of smouldering bodies. There was no area so delicate he did not risk being puerile. Once, at a party in London, catching sight of a buxom woman who choked the room with her perfume, he pointed to her, saying, '*There* is the dolphin to which we shall attach our missiles!' If the campaign began with tanks, towards the end of it, quite possibly when failure began to bite, he spoke of mysterious airships that would rise slowly from the ground, firing in all directions at once. Shortly after, he became an agent for the KGB, or so he said, although I have no reason to doubt he believed *what he believed to be the case*. Should the reader think he was wholly objectionable, the case has to be made that to those whom he liked he could be wholly likeable. A man of Swiftian wit, he could make the glasses on the table dance. As to those whom he disliked, with them he could be cruel and unreasonable.

Suddenly he closed his shop in Vancouver, transferred his stock to another bookseller, and, carrying with him a single volume of Emily Dickinson, he moved to Russia where he billeted himself with the woman who soon was to become his wife. One night, very late, he informed me on the telephone that he was going to abandon the English language and that henceforth I would have to communicate with him by means of an interpreter. Already he was growling Russian phrases at me. An old communist, he got there just in time to witness communism's demise. The pulling down of Soviet statues appalled him. Still, I believe he found happiness of a kind, not least with Masha who herself is an old communist although not a starched one. I do not remember Bill as being musically inclined but in the last year of his life, *before* he knew he was ill, he became obsessed with Mozart's *Requiem*. Although he never fully abandoned the book trade, particularly when it came to securing scarce Russian publications, another passion took over and this, which, in terms of *his* life, I found inexplicable, was the amassing of a collection of wooden toys. Together he and Masha accumulated over five thousand pieces. Scarcity and beauty were not prerequisites—they had to obtain whatever was still being made. One day, should anyone wish to know the state of Russian wooden toy production at the end of the second millennium, it will be to the apartment on Universitetsky Prospekt that he'll need to come. The shelves are banked three or four rows deep with wooden toys of every description, among them goat ladies, sawyers and blacksmiths, gentlefolk, nesting dolls, Pinocchio's, mechanical, pull and pendulum bob toys, merry-go-rounds, bird whistles, dream vehicles, red painted roosters and horses, pecking hens, bears chopping wood, bears ice-fishing, bears playing chess, fantastical *balyasy* being those gay and comical figures that spring from the minds of wits and jokers, and, moving away from the shelves, towards the ceiling, wooden birds dangling for a breeze. Their effect, en masse, is Hitchcockian.

I was trying to get a grasp on the man he had become. Admittedly, I found it difficult for he seemed to have neither the domestic nor the frivolous in him although I think he may have made heavy with both, such that his pursuit of toys became feverish in its intensity and sheer drive. What could have been his plan? I find it hard to believe he did not have one. And what of the photo of him Masha showed me, which she took late one night when he returned home, weary but ecstatic, his arms a cradle to still more wooden trophies? Who was this man for whom sentiment had been a bourgeois disease? Masha sat with her equally tall children from a previous marriage and I wondered about the Bill who with our own had been so brusque, what his relationship with them was like.

After we discussed Prokofiev and Shostakovich, the former ranking a notch above the latter in our affections, Masha asked me my opinion of Chris de Burgh. She couldn't believe I hadn't heard of him. 'But you *must* know "Moonlight and Vodka". It's wonderful! Wonderful! Listen, please.'

> That dancing girl is making eyes at me,
> I'm sure she's working for the KGB.

Chris de Burgh began to push Friar William aside in my affections.

MASHA'S TWENTY-YEAR-OLD daughter, Anya, questioned me closely on the writing of verse. She is one of those young Russian women of ferocious intelligence, who, quite unlike their more, or perhaps rather *less*, liberal sisters in the West, tilt their heads for the camera while devouring the world with their mouths and eyes.

'Why are you a poet?' she asked me. We faced each other, cross-legged on the carpet, watched by thousands of wooden eyes. I can't quite recall what I said but, worryingly perhaps, it seemed to make sense.

'What are you writing now?' I confessed that I had not written anything for quite a while.

'Why?' she demanded. Clearly, she wasn't accepting any weak excuses.

'I think I might have offended the Muse.'

'How so?'

(The wooden figurines began to whisper between themselves.)

'Well, Anya, in one of my last poems I called her a bitch.'

She stared at me, smiled faintly, and then stared some more. 'Have you not considered the possibility,' she said, 'that she *likes* being called a bitch?'

I will hazard a guess here as to the workings of the Russian psyche.

Only a *devushka*, a Muscovite too, could have said that.

The Man on the Train from Galle

Since I had peeped over the edge myself, I understand better
the meaning of his stare, that could not see the flame of the
candle, but was wide enough to embrace the whole universe,
piercing enough to penetrate all the hearts that beat in the
darkness.

—Joseph Conrad, *Heart of Darkness*

OUR TRAIN FROM GALLE to Colombo was just about
to depart when a man in his fifties, wearing a sports
jacket and flannels, with a large shaven head and
olive-coloured skin pocked all over like an avocado's, got on
and sat down in the seat diagonally opposite mine. The two
soldiers accompanying him gave a smart salute, which he
wearily returned, and then took their positions at either end
of the carriage. They propped their guns, which, with their
heavy wooden butts and lengthy barrels, seemed like armoury
from another age, against the connecting doors of the train.
The guns might have been, for all they cared, umbrellas or
garden rakes. I hoped a sudden jolt would not result in their
discharge. Almost immediately the train began to move. The
soldiers lit up cigarettes. The man in civvies I recognised from
the day before, when I saw him on Unawatuna Beach, a few
miles outside Galle. Sprawled he was and alone, on the dark

band of wet sand just where the waves broke against the shore. With each breaker he would roll once, like a beached whale, a single arm extended in a straight line. And with the next he'd roll back to where he was before. As I recall he did this for perhaps an hour or more. It was as if he had quit, for a while, the sordid business of living and had become an inanimate object wholly at the mercy of the ocean's waves. I remembered being disturbed by this, not for any reason that I could put a name to, except that his pleasure, which was of a species I had never seen before or since, seemed to come out of a terrible solitude. And now this same man, his arms folded and legs spread wide, glanced in my direction.

'You're an officer,' I said.

'A colonel,' he answered, slapping his knees. 'Come, sit here, let's talk.'

I joined him then, leaving my wife and two children on their own for the rest of the journey during the course of which, just out of the hearing of other people, the colonel and I would be oddly cocooned. I was about to enter one man's hell while, just a few feet away, my family remained in their paradise.

'You made the train just in time.'

'No, not really. I must take precautions, you see.'

I understood later that they had waited until the platform was clear and then boarded as quickly as possible. Their flurry was born of a country's bad nerves. These were dangerous times, even in such peaceful spots as the coastal town of Galle. We began with pleasantries that are of little consequence here. I told him we were catching a flight that evening to Bombay and when he expressed surprise that we wouldn't be staying in Colombo I told him we'd been there already and that we'd gone to see the house, at 8 Tickle Road, where my wife had lived when she was a small child. The colonel knew the address, which was close to his. I told him we had rung at the gate of a complete stranger's house. The Sri Lankan lady living there invited us inside, a touch puzzled to learn of the foreigners who had lived there so many years before. She knew only of the Indian family before her, about whom she was not at all polite. My wife walked through the scene of her childhood, remembering exactly where each room was. She recalled the coconut trees that still stood in a row at one edge of the garden and how she and the other children had been warned not to sit beneath them for fear of their being pummelled by falling coconuts. We went later to see the elephants at the zoo, the older of which were probably calves when, as a child, my wife was regularly taken, at four in the afternoon, to see them do their elephant dance. I did not tell the colonel of the grimmer things we'd seen in Colombo, among the darker of which was a filthy wretch at the side of a street, lying on his back in a mud puddle, a crazed look in his face, masturbating. At the train station a beggar raised his amputated arms towards our younger daughter who, never having seen such a thing before, wept and wept. Also, we had seen recently bombed sites, the consequence of the bitter war of terrorism waged by the Tamil Tigers. We knew, too, how terrible the army retribution was. I told him instead of how we'd taken the train to and from Kandy through some of the most exquisite jungle, where we saw birds of paradise. We had been to the elephant orphanage, near Kandy, where we met an elderly Sri Lankan who recited from memory 'Oh, to be in England now that April's there!' This man had loved England when he had visited it many years before although he still harboured bitter memories of being on the tube once, reading a newspaper, when a woman leaned towards him and said, 'Oh, can you read, then?' I sought to console him, saying that perhaps this was because the woman herself was illiterate. At the roadside, while waiting for a bus back to Kandy, my wife had leaned down and put her finger to a tiny fern native to this part of the world—the *nidikumba*, meaning 'sleepy plant'—whose leaves close at even the slightest touch, an action that simultaneously opened in her, as if this were some Proustian experience, a flood of childhood memories. I told the colonel what a lovely place Galle was, but I did not describe my rage of a couple of days before, when I'd witnessed a fashion shoot for one of the glossy magazines. A model in a translucent dress, with a hard and stupid face, was being positioned among 'locals', some of them very poor indeed, probably earning a pittance to look authentically native. There had been a terrible urge in me to slap her face, but then she too was a prop in a world of props where the most picturesque of all was other people's poverty. I did not tell him of the German paedophile I spoke to on Unawatuna Beach, who was quite candid about his activities and said he found this an easy country for young game. Nor did I tell the colonel that I'd seen him on the beach the day before.

A man of considerable learning, he was eager to fill any holes in my intelligence. As if he were their sole guardian he spoke to me of his country's history and culture. With pride he spoke of Sinhalese literature, in particular the sixth-century Pali chronicle, the *Mahavamsa*, which focuses on the beginnings of Sinhalese royalty and nationhood. The colonel spoke vigorously of its great battle scenes.

'Our soldiers would carry their spears like this,' he said, clutching firmly at an invisible one in front of him. 'This is how it should still be.'

'What, you'd prefer to fight with spears?' I asked.

'Yes, we might be *real* soldiers then and not what we have become. We carry instead the guns we buy from *your* people and because of them we are no longer men.'

The colonel laughed then, slapping my knees.

'So why does everybody want to sell us guns? You tell *me* why the Americans and the Russians play their games. We are their chess pieces. They play, we die. And who's to blame for this war in the first place? Why, England, of course. *You* brought the Tamils over from India to work in the tea plantations. And now, with the English gone, they demand independence. The Tamils were brought here to make the English rich and now they want part of *our* country. Does that make sense? You must return here when we are at peace. We are Buddhists, you see. We *love* peace.'

There was bitter irony in his voice. I asked him about his religion. The colonel told me he gave so much money a year to have an animal rescued from the slaughterhouse. This was not a way of atoning for one's sins nor was it the same as redemption but by doing such things, he told me, a man might ameliorate his position a little in the next life. As we spoke we entered the small coastal town of Kalutara.

'Now watch this,' he whispered to me.

The train slowed down. Suddenly the other passengers, pointing to a *Bodhi*-tree outside, bowed three times in its direction. The colonel remained rigid, his arms crossed, glaring at them with contempt.

'The fools!' he snarled. 'See what they do. And they call themselves Buddhists, when it is expressly forbidden to worship the object. Ha! What kind of Buddhism is this?'[1]

I wondered then if we had not entered a scene of spiritual warfare. Suddenly the colonel leaned forward and showed me the palms of his hands.

'What do you see in these hands?' he whispered.

A dark shadow moved across his face.

'These hands,' he repeated, 'what do you see in them?'

---

1. It would appear the colonel was much mistaken. The sacred *Bodhi*-tree (*Ficus religiosa*) is indeed an object of much reverence. The main *Bodhi*-tree in Anuradhapura, said to be the oldest tree in the world, was itself a sapling brought there from India in 306 BC, from the parent tree beneath the drooping branches of which Buddha Gautama attained Enlightenment or *nirvana*. The *Bodhi*-trees, which can be found at every major temple in Sri Lanka, are themselves mostly saplings taken from the one at Anuradhapura. The Buddha himself stated that in his absence the *Bodhi*-tree could be worshipped as *paribhogika vastu*, as something that he had made use of during his lifetime. Buddhists believe in its miraculous properties, particularly in warding off evil influence.

I said nothing, for clearly no answer was expected of me.

'Look at them carefully because now you are about to learn something. With these hands I have killed women and children.'

We sat in silence for what seemed like several minutes.

'What would you do if you were me, if you were fighting this dirty little war we've got here? I'll tell you something that happened to me. One day a pretty young woman holding a tiny baby approached two of my best officers. "Shoot her!" I shouted to them. They looked at me, one of them really confused, saying, "No, I can't!" Again I screamed, "Shoot her!" It was too late. Seconds later she, the baby and my officers were dead.'

'You mean—?'

'Yes, I *mean*.'

We sank into a deeper silence.

'What choice did I have?' he continued after a while. 'Should I have stopped to ask the woman if she had a bomb under her clothes? My officers died because they wouldn't listen to me. You see, I was a soldier once. And *now*? Now I'm a paid killer. I kill women and children. So what do I do to ease my conscience? I rescue animals from the slaughterhouse. You must listen carefully to me. I am *damned*. There will be no salvation for me, ever. I will come back in my next life as something terrible. I'll never be able to pay for my crimes. My wife in Colombo, she doesn't know any of this. I keep guards around our house at all times and she doesn't even notice they're there.'

When we arrived in Colombo we got off the train together, his guards to either side of us, their guns at the ready, their eyes alert for any untoward movement in the crowd. I asked him his name, but he waved my question away.

'No, no names,' he replied, taking my hand in his. 'When you return here one day, when we are living at peace, just ask for the colonel you met on this day on the train from Galle.'

'That will be enough?'

'Yes, it will be enough for you to be able to find me.'

I have just located my old passport so that I might check the date of our departure. The rubber stamp for embarkation is octagonal and inked in purple. Over the years, whenever I heard reports of yet more Tamil Tiger attacks on Sri Lankan government forces, I wondered if he survived them, my colonel without a name. And when I heard of Tamils being rounded up and killed, I wondered if he were in charge. I wonder now if he told many people what he told me. I think not, and for me to say so is not to wish myself into a unique position: there was something in the manner in which he spoke that would seem to indicate a man delivering himself of a terrible burden. I was someone he would never have to set eyes upon again. Clearly these were not things he could tell his wife, nor could he let his guard down with his own soldiers. Of one thing I am certain: it could not have happened anywhere other than on a train. I believe he was, at heart, a tragic figure. A single dying breath, either from one of his men or one of his victims, might have swept him over the edge. This man, who was as near as I'd ever come to meeting Mr. Kurtz in Joseph Conrad's tale, took the train from Galle to Colombo on the morning of 18 January 1986. The colonel *as* Mr. Kurtz—when I think of the fictional character I see not Brando's face in *Apocalypse Now* but his. It was a journey of almost three hours, a seemingly long ride for such a short distance.

The Master Calligrapher of Aleppo
Mohammed Imad Mahhouk

THE SLIGHT FEELING OF VERTIGO the citadel of Aleppo produces, especially at night, might just as easily be the whole of the city's past bearing down on one. History is everywhere here. There is no escaping it, not even when gossiping over tea at one of the cafés opposite. It is felt not only from above but also from beneath. 'Take care where you walk,' says the blind eleventh-century poet al-Ma'arri, 'because you walk upon the dead.' Something else he said must surely have raised a few eyes in his time: 'The inhabitants of the earth are of two sorts: those with brains, but no religion, and those with religion, but no brains.'

And still, cynic though he was, they love him. You can go and visit his tomb in Ma'arat al-Numan, a few miles south of Aleppo.

ACROSS FROM THE RISING entrance bridge to the citadel, several yards to the east, is the Madrassa as-Sultaniye, which was begun by one of Saladin's sons, Sultan al-Zaher Ghazi, and completed, after his death, in about 1225, by Ghazi's son, Governor Sultan al-Aziz. Together with the citadel in its present form, the mosque stands as a fine example of Ayyubid architecture, combining boldness and grace. It is also one of the final expressions of the glorious period initiated by Saladin, which, by 1260, soon after Ghazi's death, disintegrated in family squabbles. The *mihrab* in the prayer hall is one of the finest of its type and at the rear is a modest chamber containing the cenotaphs of Ghazi, his wife, Diafa Khatoun, and their son al-Aziz. Ayyubid power ends here, in a small room, which maybe is as it should be. After all, when the great Saladin died he did not have money enough to pay for his own funeral.

Within the madrassa's thick walls one feels locked away from the world and its vicissitudes. There is one man who has made it the condition of his working existence to be at such a remove. All night long, in a small cell off the central courtyard, the calligrapher Muhammed Imad Mahhouk pushes his reed pen until the 85-year-old caretaker arrives, dragging the sun behind him. The cell is so silent all Imad can hear are the sounds of his own breathing and the squeaking upon paper of his reed pen made from the slender thorn of the Javanese palm tree, a material noted for its durability. The reed pen (in Arabic *qalam*) is often dubbed 'the ambassador of intelligence'. The two sounds merge into one: each breath Imad takes is registered in the swell of the letters he produces.

It struck me as a perfect illustration of what the monastic life must have been like in mediaeval times. Imad agrees. 'It is the same struggle,' he says. 'It all comes from the same source—it's just a different façade. This glorious spirit is for everyone, whether it comes in the name of Islam or Christianity.' When I ask him whether he is a Sufi he says that although he belongs to no one branch of Sufism he considers himself 'a Sufi with a pen'. I ask him his age and he tells me he dates back to Ugarit, when, circa 1400 B.C., the first alphabet was produced there. Imad, in our historical time, is about fifty. Austere, he wears designer glasses; abstemious, he stops every few minutes for a smoke; disciplined, he is ramshackle as to the comings and goings of daily existence; a master calligrapher, almost incredibly he has had no master of his own.

I began by asking him how he came to be in this sacred space.

'This small room is one of many in the mosque which, of course, is already a sacred space. This was a typical old school or madrassa where young people were taught religion and sciences. The mosque no longer has the role it once had, as a university. The rooms that once housed students are now mostly used for storage. I had connections to the head of the religious board in Aleppo, which owns land and mosques. This man admired my work and at first arranged for me to have a shop at the edge of the old souq. There were too many distractions though. I would begin to write and someone would come along and interrupt me. Isolation is essential for this kind of work. So finally I was given this room for free. This space connects me to all our history and at the same time, because it is isolated behind thick walls, it keeps me away from modern society. This chamber of energy gives me peace and it has just the right atmosphere for getting into the proper mental state. I may be in isolation but I am not alone. I have no clock or watch here. I have no *time* or, rather, the only time I recognise is when I can't hold my pen anymore. My prayer mat is always next to me. Usually people pray together but because for me this space brings me even closer to the Supreme Being I prefer to pray alone. When I first enter here, I do my ablutions (*wudu*). The Qur'an must not be touched if you are unwashed. Also you must wash before prayers. I cannot start if I have not washed externally, but also I need to be internally clean, my head clear of troubles or the arguments of daily life. When I am ready, the challenge is in front of me. I know the paper's dimensions, its height and width, and yet it is almost as if I were walking into infinity. Somehow this small room gives me unlimited space in which to write. When I'm fully engaged, I do not even feel the chair beneath me. On the other hand, if I'm working on a commission and I am not interacting with the words, it can feel like a prison, as if the world has collapsed on me.'

I asked Imad what first drew him to calligraphy.

'There was no one stage or point when I decided to become a calligrapher. It was, rather, a gradual process. But to go back to the very beginnings, my father was a clerk and although he would never consider himself a calligrapher he had the most beautiful hand. My first love of calligraphy came through his writing. I was about five or six at the time. I would copy him and for me it was a fantastic game. The first beautiful thing I ever saw in my life, which I remember clearly, was the letter *wāw*, which is a circle with a tail—"و".'

There is a famous story concerning that magical letter, which may or not be true, but as an illustration of the ascent the artist makes in his striving towards God it is not surprising the story has been kept alive in calligraphic circles. What Imad told me was clearly one of several variants of the story but clinging to just one detail, which is uniquely his, I shall try to reconstruct it here from several sources. In 1258, the Mongols invaded Baghdad, slew most of the populace, and destroyed much of the city including its magnificent library, *Bayt al-Hikma* or "The House of Wisdom", which contained some of the greatest treasures of Islamic culture. They threw the books in the Tigris, so many of them that for a whole week the water was tainted with ink. It was even said that at one point in the river the volumes lay so thick the horses of the Mongols could cross over them.

Meanwhile, the city in flames, the greatest calligrapher of his time, Yaqut al-Musta'simi, hid himself away in a minaret and all he did there was to practice, in Imad's telling, the letter *wāw*. Another source says he wrote out Qur'anic verses on a piece of linen. What is indisputable is that he survived the carnage. The image of Yaqut writing at the top of a minaret, just that little bit closer to God, appears in several miniatures.

'You can spend months on a single letter,' Imad continued, 'exploring all its dimensions. I spent five or six months going around the letter *nūn*—"ن". I once heard of an imam who asked this calligrapher, "Are you going to see your lover *nūn*?" It is a delicate process. Sometimes when you stretch a letter, curve it just a bit more, you end up somewhere else, in another dimension altogether. If you want to see the beauty in calligraphy you need to come close to the letters to see how good a piece of work it is. You can *see* the calligrapher's breath, where it has been transferred to the ink, where it collects in one place or is shifted to another. You can tell how many times he held his breath before finishing a word or even a single letter. You will be able to see that he started here, went all the way and then stopped, and, in order to master the shape, went back with the finest point of the pen to produce those dark edges.'

It is almost unthinkable for a calligrapher of any standing to have *not* had the guidance of a master. One need only glance at the biographies of the great calligraphers to see that they are invariably part of a long chain of learning. As students they had to practice *taklid*, or imitation, and it is only after completing those studies that they would enter the ranks of the professionals or masters. Calligraphy, in addition to being a spiritual exercise, an emulation of the Divine, is also a precise science of geometric forms and rhythms. I asked Imad how it was he was able to make his way alone.

'Any answer to this takes me back to the 1990s, when I first went to Istanbul. It is often said the Qur'an came to the Prophet in Mecca, that it is most beautifully recited in Cairo and most beautifully written in Istanbul. Istanbul, for calligraphers, is the Mecca. It is where they all go. One of the living legends of the art is the master Hasan Çelebi, a student of Hamid Aytaç who was the greatest calligrapher of modern times, the last of the Ottoman line. When I went there my calligraphy wasn't as developed as it is now, and the techniques I employed were not those I'd use now. I had doubt in my abilities. I wasn't sure about the way I moved my pen, or even where to start and finish. Anyway I showed my work to the master Çelebi and he said to me, "What you do comes of its own accord, but at least you are doing it the right way." At same time I met another master, Nihat Çetim, and when he saw my work he said to me, "You have chosen to learn the hard way. You are like a wild herb that grows out of a rock in a harsh environment. Yes, it is a herb … yes, it is green … but in a very wild way." Actually his analogy gave me a kind of confidence. Also it provided me with a fresh perspective. The majority of calligraphers who learn directly from masters tend to block themselves. They stay in the same cast and will never escape it. If their master says a letter should be of such and such a length they will continue to make it so, but because I was in the wilderness I copied everybody. This is how I learnt, by copying every style. I'd copy even bad calligraphy. This made me flexible. When you do restoration, for example, you have to be able to *read* the other man's work and know what's bad and what's good in it and to write in exactly the same spirit as that in which he wrote. You enter another dimension, even with a bad calligrapher, and you discover things you never knew about or experienced. You can't adopt another man's style without first changing the way you hold your pen. It is like getting out of your own town and going somewhere else and then coming back to safe ground. I could see the beauty in each master's work, but at the same time I was able to make my own way. When I went to Istanbul I entered a competition they have once every three years and which is open to calligraphers from all over the world. I wanted to prove myself. I completed the piece in a day and a half, which is nothing, and got one of the main prizes. After this, I lost interest. I never went back to Istanbul. It is almost like saying I didn't need this anymore.'

'Are you considered a master now?'

'Very few people know I exist! My aim was never to achieve that role. For me, it is a natural process. It is like prayer. It is something I do.'

Salah al-Ali in his essay *Islamic Calligraphy: Sacred and Secular Writings* writes: 'The calligrapher's work lies in search of the absolute; his aim is to penetrate the sense of truth in an infinite movement so as to go beyond the existing world and thus achieve union with God.' What is produced on paper, he concludes, is as unique as the personality of whoever it is holds the reed. When speaking to Imad it is immediately clear that for him the notions of calligraphy as an art and as a form of religious devotion are inextricable. The only way he can express his special love for God, he says, is through calligraphy. What happens, I ask him, when calligraphy becomes a profession?

'The calligrapher will lose his soul, he will become as a tool. What he produces will not be art anymore. There are so-called calligraphers who write out people's names. They do not even deserve to hold a pen. One can distinguish between an artist and a craftsman. The craftsman might produce fantastic workmanship but it is not necessarily art because the love— the soul—has been lost. There has to be a balance and there have to be rules, and although calligraphy is not all that open there is freedom. A good artist will balance those two things, freedom and discipline, and still produce something new. He will go into unknown territory without disturbing the rules. Calligraphy, ultimately, is the expression of a state of mind.'

This, naturally enough, brought us to the question of spiritual revelation.

'It is quite rare, but it has happened to me several times, that when writing the Qur'an, especially a really fantastic passage, suddenly I feel this weightlessness. I'm floating. I become united with the words, or, rather, I come to the paper and see myself copying out what is already there. It's as if I am moved by a kind of fate, with the text already there, in a certain shape. My privilege is in being the first one to see it being written. There are phrases in the Qur'an, the hadith, and elsewhere which are so poetic and intense, so full of music, for example the traditional saying we have that relates to the Prophet: "You are the stranger of all the strangers."'

'It has been said that calligraphy is "the geometry of the soul." Here you are, in this very special space, where you establish a relationship between *al-qalam* "the greater, divine pen" and your own. Given that inspiration passes through the body, to what extent, then, is the physical important?'

'The soul is physically realised through calligraphy. The key to this state is the human body which is the transmitter between God and the paper. So, yes, it is a physical act and holding the reed in your hand is absolutely essential to the process, but the true nature of this relationship becomes evident on paper. It is my alibi. It is my witness. It is comparatively easy to write a single line, but to do several pages in the same style, so as to maintain a harmonious whole, this is the big challenge. There is, of course, an endless struggle between body and spirit. The spirit wants to break through the physical frame, and to expand, to reach out and to fly out of its trap, but it always hits the walls of this body and brings one down. When I'm working and get thirsty the glass of water may be just two metres away, but I won't leave my pen and paper just in order to make this body of mine shut up. I might grab a biscuit to keep me going because I don't want my body to take over. "It is not your time, it is *my* time," the soul says to it. "It is spirit time, so let me fly. I'm doing *this* now, so don't bring me down with silly needs."'

Seyyed Hossein Nasr, in his *Islamic Art and Spirituality* (Golgonooza, 1987) draws attention to the relationship between the reed as a writing implement and as a musical instrument (*ney*). 'The song of the reed,' he writes, 'is the sonoral counterpart of the letters and words of the calligrapher.' The great mystical poet Rumi invited his audience to listen to the song of the reed as it laments its separation from the reed bed. My raising the subject with Imad hit upon a happy coincidence.

'One of my friends is a great musician, and my plan is to put on a show with him playing the *ney* while I write. One will please the eye, the other the ear. The pen and the *ney* are made from the same material and in fact the word *ney* means reed. In some parts of Egypt the colloquial word for *ney* is *qassaba*, which is also the word for the throat. So there is this complex relationship whereby all these things will fit together to create a special state—the *ney* is "seen" and the pen is "heard".'

'Would you consider yourself as defending a dying art? How do you see yourself in the tradition?'

'I do not see it as a dying art because the inspiration is much stronger. The Qur'an is the main source and its strength is such that it will inspire me or someone else. There is a line in it where Allah says, "Indeed We have sent down the Qur'an, and indeed We Ourselves surely are its Guardians" [*Al-Hijr*, 15:9]. The shape of the book will never change because it is protected. It is not for anyone to alter. I am merely an instrument for bringing those words to light. The beauty of calligraphy is what enabled me *see* the Qur'an. It is what taught me how to pray, what brought me closer to God. As long as it is there, it will not be the end of calligraphy. On the other hand, life is moving so fast people do not have patience anymore and that shifts them away from such kinds of activities. There are many ways now to produce work of almost the same quality, even on computer, but it is never the same. Calligraphy is a long and complicated process, which can't be mastered in a short time. You need to have the right background, the right inspiration.'

'When you use the computer, as I believe you sometimes do, does this not go against the tradition?'

'I get cross with myself for using it, but this is merely a stage, an exploration of all the territories. I want to know everything and be everywhere. The computer is useful for technical matters—small projects, medallions, postcards, or for scanning and printing work I've already done. It could never be instrumental in creating a mental or spiritual state. Anyone can use the computer but there will never be the same quality, the same interaction. Calligraphy is calligraphy, it's sacred, whereas I might use the computer to design a pattern for a border or a background design and so rather than redo the same border a hundred times I'll do it on the computer.'

There is a striking historical analogy here, which dates from the so-called "Tulip Period" of Ottoman rule. When Ibrahim Müteferrika, a Transylvanian convert to Islam, introduced the first printing press with moveable Arabic type to Istanbul on December 14, 1727, the calligraphers, illuminators and scribes, fearful for their future, demonstrated in the streets, carrying with them a coffin filled with the implements of their trade. When the mock funeral procession arrived at the Sultanahmet Mosque, where a prayer for the dead was said, Sultan Ahmed III, who had allowed for the establishment of the printing house, asked which of the masters had died to which the response was, 'It is not the master but the mastery that has died.' Although Müteferrika's printing venture amounted to only seventeen titles, all of a non-religious nature, this marked a turning-point in the history of calligraphy. It was, one might argue, the day the 'music for the eyes' began to die. Alternatively, the advent of printing may have freed calligraphers from the drudgery of having to do things of no great artistic worth. Imad would concur with this, saying that the new technology has distinguished the real calligrapher from the one who merely writes or works on the computer. Now that things are set, he argues, calligraphy has acquired a still more prestigious status.

'So how do you see the role of the calligrapher in the modern world?'

'It has become even more important in dark and difficult times. The main thing is that I be honest about what I do. Unfortunately, in today's world, it is not enough. You need publicity … you need to be in contact with people … you need media coverage, marketing, to put these things in front of everyone. I'm incapable of this.'

Imad has produced two major works to date, the first of which is an astonishing 10.65-metre scroll, which took him a year and a half to complete, and which contains selected passages from the Qur'an including *Al-Ilkhas* ("Fidelity"), the 112th *sura* in which Allah's absolute unity is proclaimed. It is written in different calligraphic styles, ranging from the classical to the modern, all produced in miniature, and is embellished with gold. Among the scripts employed is the miniscule *al-ghubari*, which translates as 'dust-like', and is used mostly in the borders. Imad smiled at the memory of his having made it to the end without any mistakes.

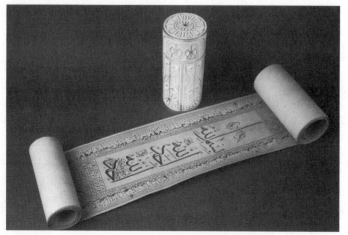

'I was so nervous doing the last twelve centimetres, which is in the *Nasta'liq* or Farsi style, so-named because it comes from Iran, and because I was in such a state it took me a whole week to write.'

'You said you managed to complete the scroll without making any mistakes, but aren't you supposed to leave an imperfection somewhere?'

'Yes, in our Islamic tradition we believe perfection comes only from God and that human beings are not capable of it. If you look at the geometric designs in a Persian carpet everything down to the smallest details is perfect, there are no mistakes, geometrically at least, but look closer and you will see the maker has intentionally left something out. After I finished the scroll I didn't feel able to carry on. I was ready to break all my pens and start on something much better, which means what I had just done was not perfect. At the beginning I was very ambitious, I put everything into it, but by the end I realised there was still so much to learn and that I would have to start all over again. It is an ever-evolving process. Another thing, and I'm talking now from the viewpoint of the observer, is that most people, because they have not had the chance to enjoy and appreciate the classical tradition, are easily impressed by phantasmagoria. Only when they have seen the right things will they see the real treasure. What you have now are people who don't have any basic knowledge or practice in real calligraphy producing things that may look impressive to those who don't know anything about how these things need to evolve. Anything new must come of real evolution. I am not after any bubble of fame.'

Also Imad completed a magnificent Qur'an in thirty sections, with only five lines to each page, its total of 15,000 lines adding up to 3000 pages. The Qur'an serves as the basis for a new project upon which he is currently working, which he reckons will take him fifteen months to complete. The identity of the person or the organisation who commissioned it remains a mystery. It will be, he tells me, the realisation of a dream project.

'I would like to think there is nothing called "calligraphy" and that there is nothing set in stone. There is only the calligrapher. As much as I appreciate the classical forms I would like to present something of my own, which is not like the script of *x* or *y* who came before, but which is my own style. What I'm doing now is inspired by a school of calligraphy that is almost forgotten, the *muhakak*, which dates mainly from the Abbasid period, but which started during the Umayyad period. The Abbasids developed it into its known shape and it was taken over, and then forgotten, by the Ottomans and then the Persians. It is the most glorious writing, with a balance between the very simple and the very complex unlike, say, the Ottoman scripts which are so complicated they become a challenge in themselves. I would like to bring this back to paper but with something of my own style. I will do something different with the *rā'* and the *wāw* and the *'alif* making them longer so as to give more elegance in the balance. I have written out the Qur'an before and the idea I had then was for it to be published but then there was some kind of problem. When I finished my first Qur'an, I had a vision of an even more beautiful script, this being the one I have just described. What I was really after is this commission, the best of the best. There were others who might have been given it, but in the end God rescued me. What is important is that whoever does this it will be impressive. An idiot will see the beauty in it. Whether he would be able to distinguish it from other works doesn't matter as this will be left for scholars to evaluate. This is a commission from God and that's the way it will be realised.'

'To what extent do you feel you'll be able to create something new?'

'I'm always accusing the schools of calligraphy, of which the Ottomans were the masters, of falling into a trap of abiding by rules they can't escape. They produce always the same shapes. Although I do not belong to any master or school, I think I am still very conservative in my approach. This is a relative matter. What is this bringing something *new* to calligraphy? Yes, I am trying to add things but I am still tied to, and have great respect for, the old teachings, the old regulations and balances. What I create is not seen by certain other calligraphers or those contemporary artists who bring calligraphy into their work as modern. They will force the letters out of shape, which for me is almost a sacrilege. You can improvise to a certain extent but you can't play with the backbone. We have already distinguished between those people who stick to the old traditions and do not move forward and those who modernise and jump about in the air whenever they think they have created something new. I do not see myself as belonging to either group. I try to be like a musician who before playing understands everything about his instrument and knows its capacities, so that it works in the way it has been designed for. What I think of as new comes naturally with things I have learned from the classical tradition. Anything additional should come according to what the tools and those teachings will allow. You don't try to play a drum with a violin, which is what some people try to do.'

When I left Imad and stepped outside, pondering whether such a combination was possible, the moon over the citadel opposite signalled bedtime for me but for the master calligrapher of Aleppo it meant only the beginning of another night's work.

Zoroaster's Children

1

AT THE MAIN BUS STATION in Tehran, a shabbily dressed man stopped in front of me and ran a finger across his throat. 'Iran no good,' he whispered. I wanted to ask him why, find out what his story was, but already he was gone. All I can remember now is a terrible blankness in his face and then the back of his head as he slipped into the crowd until, seconds later, I could no longer tell which one was his. Almost exactly the same thing would happen to me in Isfahan—a scarecrow of a figure standing beneath a concrete bridge—same words, same gesture. When I stopped to say hello, pretending I hadn't understood him, he repeated the sentence over and over, as if it were a mantra drained of significance, his deadened eyes fixed upon some point further than I'd ever be able to see.

Should one describe a country in terms of its extremes? I could just as easily have begun by relating any number of kindnesses, but even these, as I moved from formal pleasantries to serious discourse, often had their sorrowful edges. Although my journey would take me, in a sense, from darkness towards light, what struck me most about the Iranians was their tragic demeanour. They seem to lack what the Arabs have in abundance—a sense of irony, and with it a capacity for easy laughter—they suffer endlessly, deep within themselves. 'One does not laugh too loudly here,' I was told, 'for fear of upsetting one's neighbour.' If a cold shaft of steel runs through people's lives, this is not at odds with their extraordinary hospitality—rather, it serves to explain it, as if there were nothing else to do but huddle together for warmth before a small fire.

Nearly the whole of history has been, as contemporary Iranians see it, one blow after another. One can almost smell the tears on the breeze. *Still* they speak of invasions, first that of the Arabs, this uncouth desert people who brought with them, on the tip of a sword, their new and majestic faith. I met even devout Muslims who spoke of the Arab invasions with more than a tinge of regret in their voices. They complained of how heavily their neighbours, destroying everything as they went, had struck at the Persian psyche. 'The Arabs, even now, refer to us as *ajam* ("they who do not speak the language").' At the same time they boasted of having given the Arabs, in their architecture and literature, the greater culture. There is a sense, though, in which the winged symbol of Ahura Mazda still hovers above the people. A merchant in Shiraz told me, 'Scratch any Iranian and you'll find a Zoroastrian beneath the skin.' I think this helps explain why in a country that has so often persecuted religious minorities, particularly the Baha'is, the surviving Zoroastrians have been given more latitude than most. If the Muslims are tolerant of the Zoroastrians it is perhaps because they remember what they themselves once were.

Some six hundred years after the Arabs came the first of the Mongol hordes. A shudder runs through people when they speak of this. Almost the entire population of Isfahan was slaughtered by Tamerlane, who had the skulls of his victims heaped in pyramids. The Orient is a place where news stays news, something that we in the West ought to bear in mind when scratching our heads at, or when seeking to remedy, ancient grievances. The Iranians are quick to see imperialistic designs in every movement, in every shade. Another merchant spoke, almost with admiration, of the English, whom he feared for their intelligence more than he did the Americans, who, he said, are more honest but infinitely more naïve. 'A hundred years ago, the English gave us the opium trade,' he laughed, 'and now there are warehouses in Isfahan full of the stuff, all of it destined for Europe.'

Far more recently, of course, came the Islamic Revolution, when corpses dangled from cranes. 'It was something we did in a terrible moment of drunkenness, out of some misdirected sense of hope,' a cabdriver told me. 'By the time we sobered up it was too late.' It is curious how in a country where alcohol is proscribed the most common analogy, in both poetry and ordinary parlance, is that of wine and its effects.

> Can drunkenness be linked to piety
>> And good repute?
> Where is the preacher's holy monody,
>> Where is the lute?

There are even those who, in speaking of this 'terrible moment', would rather put the blame anywhere other than upon themselves, and claim that the Americans installed the Ayatollah Khomeini in revenge for the Shah having bitten their hand on the matter of oil prices. Anything's possible—there is no theory too fantastic in the Orient, none that can't be supported by a thousand lesser truths. Real enough, though, have been the horrors endured by ordinary people. During the war with Iraq, which most people I spoke to still believe the West helped engineer—back then Iran rather than Iraq was held to be the most evil of countries—barely a family did not suffer the loss of a father, brother, or son. A woman who worked at the front, recycling the uniforms of dead soldiers, described to me how once when she lifted a tunic from a pile of soiled clothes a severed hand dropped out of a sleeve. She told me how young children were used to clear landmines. Clutching olive branches, singing religious songs, and believing what the mullahs told them, that soon they'd be in Paradise, they would walk until they stepped on a mine. 'And do you want to know something really terrible,' she said. 'I envied them. God help me, I deeply envied those children and their martyrdom.'

These are only some of the things that I was told. They make for a patchwork of mostly dark hues, as if the brighter fabrics of Iran's magnificent culture have come to count for little. Depression, though, implies loss of perspective. At the same time Iranians are deeply sensitive to the picture of them presented by the world outside. Their natural reluctance to be judged by their regime is such that they will actually defend it at times. Any creature forced into a corner bristles. There is, on the other hand, a tendency in the Orient for people to follow their rulers no matter how ruthless they are. Another man I spoke to described it thus: 'In ancient Persian belief, certain men were believed to possess a divine ability to govern people, which was called *farr-é izadi* or "heavenly light". The king was considered a shadow of the god. What is the business of his subjects, then, but to gather in this shadow? We have now one supreme leader, but this is something much older than Islam.' A woman of cool intelligence asked me, faintly smiling, how it was that the most powerful people in the world had only Bush and Gore to choose between, whereas they, one of the weaker peoples, had elected a trained philosopher.

One can also look upon contemporary Iranians as part of some everlasting procession. At the ruins of the Apadana Palace at Persepolis, I was numbed by the seemingly endless sequence of sculpted figures, all marching in the same direction, from staircase to staircase, each barely distinguishable from its neighbour. There is nothing in those bas-reliefs of the warmth or spontaneous movement that one finds in ancient Greek sculpture. The figures are almost all functionaries—nobles, foreign dignitaries, soldiers, and vassals from conquered countries, bearing offerings to the king. They move as might stone through stone, in silence. Or so it seemed until I paused at one turning of the staircase, where, to my surprise, I found a sudden break in the pattern. There were just two figures, one of whom has stopped and turned to converse with his neighbour, and together they stand in eternal dialogue, at this blind spot, where nobody else in the grim, bearded parade can see them. Was there not on the part of the sculptor some unconscious message here?

During the three weeks I spent in Iran, I met, as has so often been my good fortune, people who guided me over and beneath surfaces, and with whom I spoke as I imagine those two ancient figures spoke, in low voices. What I hope to describe here are some of those conversations, unheard by religious or secular police, in which hearts suddenly opened and just as quickly closed.

2

I arrived in Isfahan in the middle of a terrible drought; for the first time in ages the Zayandé Rud, 'The River of Life,' was dry as a bone. Women in their black chadors, to get from one side of town to the other, took shortcuts across the riverbed, which looked like a desert scene dropped in the middle of an urban one. I drank tea at a wonderful *chaykhané* built into the base of the old Si o Sé Bridge, but it was without the pleasure of watching moonlight dance on the water or of hearing waves slap to the drum tap of a Persian tune. A man at a neighbouring table said the Iranian people were being punished for their crimes. 'When people lie, cheat, and murder it doesn't rain.

The country itself is being punished.' Clearly, an ancient god was showing his displeasure.

One of the first things I did was stop at a bookshop to ask if there were any translations of the poet Ahmad Shamloo available. This was not as unlikely as an Iranian in London finding a Persian edition of Ted Hughes, but it was improbable all the same. Admittedly, though, I had a hunch that my enquiry might open up the city and its culture for me. I've been served well by such gambits in the past, as when in Damascus I asked after the poet Muhammad al-Maghut, which finally led to my meeting him. This would not be the case with Shamloo who had died a few months earlier. Indeed I knew nothing of him other than the fact that many young Iranians admired his verses. My impression, or rather the one that had been fed me, was of a poet more powerful than the regime that sought to contain him, and who, in images that slipped the notice of the censors, or that the censors *allowed* to slip their notice, addressed current problems yet managed to remain within a strong lyrical tradition. I knew, too, that people in the East are usually keen to oblige when a foreigner shows an interest in their culture.

A young man, at that very moment buying a number of books, looked up in surprise and pointed to the thin volume on top of his pile, which turned out to be none other than Shamloo's last, posthumously published, collection. 'Shamloo is my favourite contemporary poet,' he said, 'but translation into English? No, no, I think that would be impossible. There are so many double and even *triple* meanings in the words he uses. When, just a few months ago, I heard the news of his death I cried. I felt something pulled away from me. Later on, I learned that just ten minutes before he died Shamloo called for pen and paper and wrote his last poem, about there being no need to fear death.'

Farhad, as he introduced himself to me, then spoke of his love for English literature, in particular Virginia Woolf's *To the Lighthouse.* I hedged a little, not so much because I dislike her but because as a bookseller then working in Bloomsbury I suffered overly from Woolf Syndrome, having been asked too many times by too many gleaming faces for the address where she lived. I just wasn't prepared to countenance her in Isfahan. Farhad seemed shocked that I was unable to share his enthusiasm.

'The second chapter of that book,' he told me, 'presents a picture of solitude that makes me weep every time I read it. Also, have you read Michael Cunningham's *The Hours*, which is partly based on *Mrs. Dalloway*? It is a masterpiece.'

We agreed to meet the following day.

I SPENT THE FOLLOWING MORNING in Emam Khomeini Square and the Great Bazaar. A century ago, the first thing a traveller approaching Isfahan would have seen was the blue dome of the mosque, the Masjed-é Emam (or the Masjed-é Shah as it was then known), whereas now one goes through miles of nondescript buildings, and one must come very close indeed before seeing anything of the town's glories. Once inside the huge square, however, one can see nothing of the surrounding modern city, only the tops of the mountains to the south and blue skies. It is as if the ancient heart of Isfahan were one great conjuring trick and the two worlds, old and new, mutually exclusive. I wonder to what extent this describes the traveller's perspective in general.

I visited just about everywhere, carrying Robert Byron's *The Road to Oxiana*, and was more impressed than ever by the conciseness of his observations. On the matter of architecture, I have nothing to add to anything he wrote. Still, Byron's is only a partial picture. There is little room in his writing, superb though it is, for spiritual significance. I recommend that a traveller also take with him Seyyed Hossein Nasr's *Islamic Art and Spirituality*. Nasr chooses for his epigraph Ya Karim's 'God has

inscribed beauty upon all things.' While Byron, an aesthete
of the first order, marvels at the end products, Nasr stands at
the beginning to all such discussion. All I will say, as a statement of my own preferences, is that I was much more deeply
moved by the Masjed-é Sheikh Lotfollah than by its grandiose
neighbour, the more photogenic but, to my careless heart and
untrained eye, less spiritually rich of the two. Happily, and
with words I myself could never conjure, Byron supports me.
I say this although it was the blue tiles of the Emam Mosque
that first drew me to Isfahan. Suddenly they had become too
pretty for my taste.

THAT EVENING FARHAD INVITED ME back to his place, not far
from Emam Khomeini Square, for he wanted me to see his
library. His father, a carpet merchant, had died a few years
earlier, and now Farhad, who had no intention of taking on
the family business, was living off his inheritance. What he
wanted more than anything, as a kind of defence against the
world outside, was to build for himself a library of books in
English. As I looked at the neat rows of ordinary paperbacks—
and there weren't so many of them really—I had the sense
that this indeed was a great collection, that I who dealt in rare
books had never seen any quite so rare as these.

'You can't imagine the difficulty I had in obtaining some of
them.'

These were books one could buy anywhere in London.
I pondered the difficulties I had had in finding obscure
titles, and yet how spoiled for choice I had become. Farhad
opened a book and began to recite "The Love Song of J.
Alfred Prufrock", not as so many people studying English
in the Orient do, by rote, but rather with a perfect feel for
the poem. The old paperback trembled in his hands. The
poem was, he explained to me, a mirror held up to his own
painful existence.

'The only difference between Mr. Prufrock and myself is that I do not keep my trouser legs rolled up.'

I asked him what he was going to do when, as he had predicted would happen in two or three years' time, he reached the end of his inheritance.

'Oh, that's easy,' he replied. 'There will be nothing left for me other than suicide. Until then, these books will be my escape.'

'In that case, Farhad, they will have failed in their purpose.'

'What do you mean?'

'I mean, that if you commit suicide then you will have ignored the most important message contained in all these volumes.'

'Which is?'

'Which is *to live*.'

I have learned that when east of the Mediterranean one must sometimes reach for such rhetorical extravagances—one must be passionate. Farhad sat in a troubled silence for a while.

'Do you like Isfahan?' he asked me.

I produced the obvious answer, which, I believe, he expected of me. I had had my fun earlier that day, in a carpet shop where somebody asked me what I thought of his country. 'Awful,' I said. He translated for his friends who stared at me in amazement. He then asked what I thought of the Iranian people. 'They're even worse,' I replied. Again he translated, and the group burst into wild applause.

'Yes,' Farhad said, 'it's one of the world's more beautiful prisons.'

I asked him to describe this beautiful prison.

'Each day I look into the mirror this city is and I see only my own distorted face, unrecognizable to myself, and I wish to go somewhere where I might be able to break the mirror. I want, above all, to escape the hypocrisy of this country, where everything, even love, is hidden behind a curtain. It has got so I cannot believe even in love and prefer, or perhaps have no option for myself other than, solitude. There is, you see, this dominant sadness in my people, which has been there throughout their history and which is reflected in the music and poetry. Look, I love this country, its history and its culture, but I am prepared to leave it forever.'

If English literature was Farhad's first escape route, music was his second.

'You will find in both our music and poetry a constant theme, which is of separation, the separation between lovers and the separation within ourselves.'

We listened to the music of Gholam Hussein Banan, in particular his ravishing rendition of *Elaheh Naz*, with lyrics by the poet Karim Fakoor. A kind of spiritual anthem to many Iranians, it is, to my Western ears, suggestive of Humphrey Bogart, women with feathered turbans and deep cleavages, villains with slicked-back hair and fruity voices, and doubtful fumes. Farhad then played for me some Mohammad Reza Shajarian, Iran's greatest living exponent of traditional or classical music. Where Banan evoked subterranean darkness, Shajarian produced a light too powerful for the naked eye.

The following day Farhad did not show up for our scheduled meeting. I waited and waited, and although not wholly surprised I was disappointed. I concluded that by speaking to me he had opened the gates of his despair a bit too wide.

A COUPLE OF DAYS LATER, towards evening, the streets filled with people celebrating the festival of Eid and what they hoped was the imminent return of the twelfth imam. The last direct descendant of the Prophet, via his daughter Fatima and his son-in-law Ali, the twelfth imam ('the Guided One', 'the Lord of the Age', 'the Awaited One', 'the Hidden One') is said to have disappeared when he was five. The belief is that he is still alive somewhere. Towards the end of time—that is, shortly before the Day of Judgement—he will return as *mahdi* to restore order and justice to the world. 'They might just as well wait for Santa Claus,' a cynic told me. Still, it was an occasion on which the youths in particular went wild, shouting, laughing, and throwing firecrackers. Shopkeepers put out cakes for people to help themselves from, and soup was being ladled out at street corners. It was a kind of mass drunkenness, without the alcohol perhaps, but not without a degree of menace.

I was pushing through the throng when a girl, her pale face bright in her black chador, called out my name. I stood there, utterly perplexed. 'Marius, remember me? It's Tonye. Remember, al-Haramain?' I could hardly believe my eyes, for it was a Norwegian girl who had stayed at the same hotel as I in Damascus a couple of years before and with whom I had pleasant chats almost every evening. Tonye hardly ever ventured out of doors, for she had decided to study for her university exams in a hotel far from home. Indeed her discipline was most remarkable—as soon as our talks came to an end she would return to the books she always had at her side. She was not easily identifiable in a chador. Unthinkingly, I embraced her and kissed her on both cheeks, realising too late my terrible mistake. Such public displays of affection are thoroughly frowned upon in the Muslim world, particularly in Iran, and before I could back away from her we were descended upon by a mob of youths. The next thing I knew I was on the ground, some boys screaming in my face and mock-kissing me. When I fought my way free I found Tonye had been similarly attacked, the youths pulling at her clothes and grabbing her all over. A boy of about ten reached between her legs. I rushed towards her, but already a group of older males were stopping the assault. We were rushed up a flight of stairs into someone's office, where we hid until the mob dispersed.

'You see,' our rescuer explained, 'how they are, how frustrated they have been made. At moments like this they completely lose their sanity.'

85

This, after all, was a country where the natural modesty of Muslims was being enforced as with a sledgehammer, where even a boy and a girl talking on a street corner, if they weren't brother and sister, could be interrogated by the *komité*, the religious police. Where in the Qur'an are the passages to support this? I felt terrible, of course, about having provoked this attack, and although Tonye accepted my apologies with considerable grace it was the last time I saw her.

I didn't feel I could leave Isfahan without at least saying goodbye to Farhad, who, when I phoned him, pleaded a cold and offered profuse apologies for his earlier non-appearance. An hour later, we sat on riverside rocks, staring at the cracked bed of the Zayandé, on whose banks, prior to the earthquake of 1853, one could smell the roses.

> I think on them whose rose gardens are set
> Beside the Zindeh Rud, and I forget
> Life's misery.

I ran through my fingers the string of worry beads Farhad had given me as a parting gift. Music drifted down from the *chaykhuné* at the Si o Sé Bridge. I could tell there was something he wanted to say to me, in private, which was why he had chosen this secluded spot.

'There is a line in one of Ahmad Shamloo's poems, "You smell my breath." This is not something you can translate, that would make any sense on its own. You would never guess what that line refers to, and there's nothing in your culture that would make it translatable. A few years ago, when I was a university student in Shiraz, I went to visit my professor at his house. I was working on an assignment, and he was giving me some tutorial advice. When we'd finished he asked me if I would like to try some gin. I said "Yes, why not?" and he poured me a bit at the bottom of a glass, about half an inch or so, certainly not enough to make me drunk. Actually it had no effect on me whatsoever. We concluded our discussion and I left his place. Almost immediately, in the darkness, a policeman came up to me and, as they do here, put his nose to my mouth and did like this.'

Farhad sniffed twice, like a Pekinese.

'"You've been drinking!" the policeman shouted at me. What could I do? I didn't want to get my professor into trouble. I was arrested and taken to prison, a minuscule cell where there must have been about twenty people squeezed inside. You can imagine the filth, the shit and piss. Among my cellmates were some of the lowest of the low—rapists, thieves. Others were there for only the smallest crimes. There was one man who had been arrested for possessing a satellite dish. The next day I was taken to court, unwashed and unshaven, and there the mullah harangued and insulted me, saying he would write a letter to my university, demanding that I be dismissed. This was terrible, the worst possible thing that could happen to me. So what did I do? I got down on my knees before the mullah and, I'm ashamed to say, pleaded with him: "Please, I beg you, *anything* but that." The mullah laughed. "Take him away for punishment, then." This was the alternative course and, in truth, I was relieved. I was taken to a room where I was stripped naked, placed over a barrel, and two men took turns whipping me. I was given eighty-four lashes. I could hear my own screams as if they were somebody else's and even see the blood, *my* blood, flying through the air over my head. My poor mother came to collect me. I was unable to move, and for the next two weeks I lay face down on a bed while she poured oils into my raw flesh.'

I saw something terrible in Farhad's eyes, not just the tears that gathered there, but also the gaping hole this experience had burned into his youth, which nothing could ever fill.

'I will tell you something. The physical healing comes soon enough. But this,' he said, pointing to his head, 'this is never cured.'

I thought of the madman I'd seen under the bridge a few days before, running his finger across his throat and the man at the bus station in Tehran. Farhad stared ahead in silence for the longest time.

'The river is empty,' he said at last, 'and so too is the soul of this country.'

3

The journey from Isfahan to Yazd takes one through one of the bleakest landscapes imaginable, resembling an endless stretch of unbaked clay with precious little to which a wandering mind may attach itself. I, who normally love deserts, did not appreciate this one. Who could live in such a forbidding place other than the foul-tempered scorpions, tarantulas and snakes that make it their home? But Yazd itself is fascinating, with its adobe architecture and wind-towers (*badgirs*) atop many of the wealthier houses. These marvellous structures feature small sticks that rake the skies for the slightest draft, which is then drawn through vents and down an inner shaft, creating a current that, by the time it reaches the bottom, has become a cooling breeze; to me they epitomise human ingenuity in its purest form. Though not as cheering, a further instance of the Persian genius for survival, which borders on the poetic, is the *ghanats*, underground water channels, some of which are over two thousand years old and a hundred metres deep. The mathematics required to link underground water supplies separated by many miles is almost inconceivable, and so perilous was the construction of the *ghanats* that many workers breathed their last burrowing deep beneath the desert surface.

On the outskirts of Yazd, in a small side street, I was tempted to knock on a door with a sign that read, in English, 'The Institute for Living in Harmony with the Desert.' Instead I made for the Towers of Silence (*Dakmeh*), hill-top enclosures where, until they were forced to abandon the custom some thirty years ago, Zoroastrians used to leave their dead to be picked over by vultures. (Now the deceased are buried in the modern cemetery nearby, in tombs lined with brick or cement so as to avoid any contact with the contaminating earth.) I climbed to the top of one of the towers and crawled through a small entrance into a flat area at whose centre was a pit into which, after the vultures had done their work, the bones would be pushed. But the last thing one could hope for at the Towers of Silence was silence, for young daredevils, wasting time and brains, ran their motorbikes up and down the slopes all day long.

All the Muslims I spoke to expressed affection for the Zoroastrians. Such feelings were not extended to the Ba'hais, who, being neither Sunni nor Shi'ite, were considered to be nothing at all. The Ba'hais view their faith as a purified form of Islam, which is enough to raise the hackles of the religious mainstream, but the strength of the prejudice against them remains inexplicable. It was the same hostility that Edward Granville Browne wrote about in his 1893 masterpiece, *A Year Among the Persians*, except that now the few Ba'hais who have stayed on in the country have made themselves even more invisible. They are cursed even in their absence. Only one person I met described them as a gentle people—others with whom I raised the issue were close to inarticulate with hate. The Zoroastrians, on the other hand, were 'honest', 'hard-working', 'reliable' and so on. This would surprise some of the Zoroastrians I spoke to, who considered themselves victimised. Others I met either felt happy enough to blend in with the Muslim populace or, more likely, did not wish to compromise themselves. (A stranger is not entitled to opinions people are loath to express even between themselves.)

When I visited the Zoroastrian Fire Temple (*Ateshkadé*) and stared into the sacred flame that, so one is told, has been burning continuously since the fifth century, lit at a point when the religion was already a thousand years old, I couldn't help but feel that here was the isthmus of a scarcely imaginable past reaching into the present, the winged symbol of Ahura Mazda, belonging not to this but to a world of carved stone.

I struck up a strange friendship with a man I never really got to speak to. The absence of a translator, though, was never a bar to communication. Although Reza hardly ever smiled, I would not say he was miserable. I think he was just deeply serious, as if in the middle of some philosophical problem he would never live long enough to solve. This brooding aspect was the first thing I noticed when I saw him walking alone, up and down an alley in the empty bazaar, apparently with nothing to do, nowhere to go, and nobody to see. Reza nodded and, summoning me over, took a key from his pocket and opened one of the painted steel doors that line the alleys of the bazaar. I found myself inside a dark cave of a place, which turned out to be his father's dyeing workshop. Reza showed me the various processes used in dyeing wool, then signalled to me to follow him up a ladder and through a small door that gave onto the vast roof of the bazaar where the newly dyed wool was hung to dry. The adobe architecture of Yazd is never more remarkable than when seen from this vantage, the undulating surface broken by holes through which one may peer down into the alleys below.

Suddenly Reza began to sing in the traditional Persian fashion, with an occasional ululation in the throat, achieved by pressing and jiggling a couple of fingers there. The sun was going down, and Reza sang what I took to be a lament, which could surely be heard for over a mile. Listening to him up there on the strange adobe roof was like being on another planet, and made for the most magical moment of my journey so far.

That evening I wandered into a subterranean teahouse, a magnificent place with pools beside which people squatted in alcoves, smoking their water pipes. Suddenly the talking stopped and the air filled with a familiar voice. I learned then that the man who had serenaded me earlier was the poet-singer of Yazd. I asked him if he would be my guest for supper, and he accepted with a faint smile. We ate in a brooding silence.

The next morning, as the bus left for Shiraz, there was a sudden downpour. I remembered the words of the man at the *chaykhuné* in Isfahan and fancied that an ancient god's forgiveness might have had something to do with a song thrown at the skies.

4

THERE'S A SENSE in which Aramgah-é Hafez, the garden that contains Hafez's tomb, *is* Shiraz. It would just be another city otherwise, pretty enough in parts, drearily modern in the main, with far too little evidence of its former architectural glories. The reason why even snooty Isfahanis cite Shiraz as their favourite place is that it is home to the poet who addresses them from beyond the grave. Hafez draws unto himself the aspirations of a whole people. A story, perhaps true, concerns a meeting between Hafez and Tamerlane who, despite his savage treatment of conquered peoples, was not wholly blind to their poetic qualities. The poet had been in arrears with his taxes. Tamerlane quoted to him one of his own lines, in which Hafez writes of his beloved that he would trade Bukhara and Samarkand for the mole on her face. 'A man prepared to barter like this,' remarked the tyrant, 'with those very cities that are mine, must surely be able to pay his taxes.' Hafez replied that it was on account of such reckless generosity that he was bankrupt. Tamerlane, much pleased with this response, sent him away with a gift—one wonders if Hafez had to pawn it in order to pay his taxes. As an illustration of the poet's character the story *feels* true and in the Orient such embellishments should not always be viewed as false any more than in the West our candour should always be taken at face value.

Not even Shakespeare and Dante are as *revered* in our world as Hafez is in his. It is no exaggeration to say that Hafez is almost an alternative religion. According to another legend, when he died, in 1389, religious elders were unsure whether he should be accorded a Muslim burial. After all, the deceased would appear to have imbibed more than just spiritual wine. The extraordinary thing is that the elders, in seeking to resolve the problem of his internment, consulted his verses, which may be one of the earliest instances of Hafez's *Divan* being used for purposes of divination. The oracle was consulted and the oracle replied:

> And when the spirit of Hafez has fled,
> Follow his bier with a tribute of sighs;
> Though the ocean of sin has closed o'er his head,
> He may find a place in God's Paradise.

The poet was buried in the place of his choice, Mosalla, and there he remains, within the mandala of his octagonal shrine, a rebuff to all those of religious extremes. This is not to say that he, or rather his verses, did not suffer further persecution. An account, dating from the eighteenth century, speaks of a proposed *fatwa* against his writings. Luckily the decision was put in the hands of a leading cleric, who, in his wisdom, decided that although Hafez's poetry was subject to interpretation of an indecent nature there was nothing morally suspect in the verses themselves.

Hafez suffered badly at the hands of his first English translators until he was delivered from them by Gertrude Bell in 1897 and, a few years later, more obscurely, by Elizabeth Daryush in her several lovely versions. But nothing matches the horrors visited upon him in recent years. There has been a New Age tendency, with both Rumi and Hafez, to make soft and blur the edges of the very thing that most demands our discipline. Only recently, in my reading, did I suffer from yet another dose of Hafez served up as Persian soufflé. This is the powdered mysticism to which we are invited to add water and stir once.[1] One is made to forget just how rooted in the real world Hafez's poetry is, and how often, with him, the satirical cuts through the ethereal. Hafez could not abide hypocrites: 'The ascetic,' he wrote, 'is the serpent of the age.' Also, *form* is integral to his vision, and even the best English translations are at best approximate. Hafez is, by and large, a poet we have to take on trust. I write this fully aware of how difficult it is to translate my own experiences of him into something not perilously close to that which I scorn. True mysticism, though, cuts like a blade. There is no doubt whatsoever that for many Iranians their experience of him is a mystical one.

It was at Aramgāh-é Hafez, amid the orange trees, with Mohammad Reza Shajarian's renditions of Hafez, Sa'di and Khayyám playing in the background, that I spent much of my time. A whole book could be written on meetings with people there. This is not a tomb upon which one casts a cold eye, and I daresay the small area surrounding it is the freest place in Iran. It is where people divest themselves of the burden of sorrow and where, especially in the case of the women, those otherwise dark bundles of silence, eroticism is given temporary clearance.

> When I am dead, open my grave and see
> The cloud of smoke that rises round thy feet:
> In my dead heart the fire still burns for thee.

---

1 Happily, with the recent publication of Dick Davis's superb translation *Faces of Love – Hafez and the Poets of Shiraz* (Penguin Books, 2013), this is no longer the case.

An elderly *seyed* and his friend, a young man on crutches, both with some difficulty fell to their knees, their foreheads touching the ground, and there they remained for some time. They had travelled all the way from Kabul to Shiraz just so they might pay their respects to the man who for them is the world's greatest poet. They invited me to photograph them, as if they wanted somebody in the world to have evidence of their difficult pilgrimage. Then came a boxer with a broken nose, who had come from Mashhad, together with his pretty fiancée. We spoke of Hafez, but he was more eager to learn how he might obtain copies of *The Ring*, an American boxing magazine, and then, on learning I had come from England, he extolled Henry Cooper, who, even if he didn't win, had at least managed to knock down Muhammad Ali. All this might have seemed inappropriate at the tomb of Hafez, but boxing, he told me, was not so much a sport as an art, one that he had inherited from his father, who also was a boxer and his coach.

A young poet I spoke to, Daryush Mehboody, described his own work as being in a polyphonic style, with leanings towards Rimbaud and Apollinaire. Already the author of a couple of books, he seemed serious enough, although I worried a little when he described one of his poems as comprising a dialogue between Hitler and Oedipus, whom he took to be two sides of the same coin. Mehboody had recently completed a new work, written in two columns, the one on the left being a commentary on the ode to the right of it, which, when read in tandem, made a poetic whole. I asked him if he were *avant-garde*. This two-column form, he told me, was to be found in early Persian writings. When I raised the subject of Hafez he asked me if I believed in magic.

'This mausoleum is a metaphysical space. Strange things happen here. It is the moment when art begins, when music, for instance, gives expression to feelings we cannot express otherwise, which is why, of course, some religious people fear music. There are certain affections in the universe we connect to. Say I live in a house that has something very special in it, a calming effect. If one person were to say this you might believe him—if two, then you'd believe a bit more; but when many people say this, you begin to accept that it's true. And so it is with the tomb of Hafez: so much happens within this space. The shrine, as you see, has eight sides, is an octagon, a mandala, and in Jung's psychology this is a holy form.'

He wrote in my notebook a quotation from Hafez, 'With your dark eye you have infiltrated my religion a thousand times. Come, let me remove a thousand illnesses from your eyes.' I wondered what those illnesses were meant to be.

A CANARY SANG FROM A CAGE hanging from a cypress tree and a wasp danced about my head, its flight in perfect harmony with the sound of the *ney*, the Oriental flute. A young man invited me back to his table, where there were several people, including his sister, Azadeh, an intense and attractive young woman. She followed our conversation in studious silence. A dervish with a long white beard and dressed in brown robes sat at a neighbouring table. We invited him to join us. A *majnun* or 'holy fool', he told us he had witnessed much pain and cruelty in this life but that he had found an escape.

'When you get to know God you disappear in the world.'

'What can you tell me about Khizr?'

Khizr (or the Arabic 'Khidr') had fascinated me ever since I first learned about him in Damascus, where he is identified with the Christian St. George almost to the point of being interchangeable with him. Khizr is also synonymous with the Jewish Elijah and in European mythology becomes the Green Man. Although he is never named in the Qur'an, Muslims will tell you that it is he who accompanies the prophet Moses on his journeys. As a figure of fecundity and rebirth he would appear to predate all three great monotheisms. The paths between cultures have been overgrown with ignorance, but as a single meeting point for all three there is no figure that cries out more for our attention. Where Khizr differs from the martyred St. George is in the fact that he drank from the waters of immortality, and thus remains the living presence to whom many Muslim mystics have turned for guidance. Hafez attributed his poetic gift to a meeting with Khizr.

'Khizr is wherever you need him to be,' the dervish told me, 'and whomever you wish him to be, whether as teacher or guide, and in whatever religion, in whatever form he takes. You have to find him. He is in the world. In any decade, any country, Khizr will always be there.'

'And did you find him?'

'Yes, that's why I'm a *majnun*. All dervishes have seen Khizr. Night after night, he gave me messages. People say God is bright, but one cannot compare him with anything that we see. I've been a *majnun* for twenty-six years.'

Azadeh stared at me from the other end of the table in surprise.

'How do you know so much about our religion?' she asked.

I was startled to hear her clear English sentence coming, as it were, from a hitherto deep silence.

'I know very little, but I am interested in that particular figure.'

Azadeh looked at me sceptically, saying, 'I think you know more than you wish to admit.'

On the basis of a scrap of knowledge she seemed to think I knew everything about her faith and asked me to compare it with Christianity. Which, she asked me, was the better of the two? This, I replied, was a question that need not concern us here, not where one man's poetry healed the divisions between people. We spoke across the length of that table, a few heads to either side of it, and without too much trouble managed to dissolve the distance between us. Afterwards, we strolled over to the tomb of Hafez. We watched a young woman fall to her knees, and, after first knocking at it three times, kiss the edge of the tomb and then place her cheek on the marble. She ran her fingers through the rose blossoms scattered there. It was almost as if she were physically caressing the spirit inside. The woman was so completely transported I doubt she was aware of our presence.

'You see,' Azadeh whispered, 'she believes in Hafez. She has come to confide in him all her hopes so that he, in his wisdom, might see them fulfilled.'

'Why did she knock three times?'

'She was saying hello to Hafez, and that she hopes this is a nice place for him, and that his soul is with God.'

When I asked Azadeh if she thought the woman was in love, she was terse in her response.

'There are so many things I wish I could tell you.'

At that moment, the woman kneeling at the tomb and Azadeh, both of them all in black, seemed to merge into a single being. It was one of the most disturbingly beautiful things I've seen, a display of sensuality that here, in a country where such things were forbidden, unsettled me.

Later, as her brother drove us around Shiraz, I told Azadeh about my maternal ancestor in the East India Company and his harem of thirteen wives, one of whom was called Beebee Mahrattun al-Nifsa Begume.

'She is your ancestor?'

'With a name like that, I hope so.'

'Oh, my God,' Azadeh cried, doubled over with laughter, 'you're one of us! Good, good! So now I'll give you your Muslim name, Abul Fazd, which means "the father of all things nice and good".'

In a surprisingly husky but tender voice, she sang a song, which she then translated for me.

'*I shed tears enough to fill an ocean … ,*' it began.

We arrived at her family home.

'Come,' she said, fleeing up some outdoor stairs. We found ourselves on the roof, standing several feet apart. 'Come closer,' she said, 'don't be afraid.' We stood in silence, looking at the stars. She pointed to the courtyard below.

'See, that's where we sleep during the hot summer nights.' Suddenly she turned to me. 'I like you because you are romantic, and I am too.'

I was surprised by her directness. I asked her if her hair was long or short and she told me it went down to the small of her back.

'Why hide it?' I asked, although I already knew the answer.

'The Qur'an forbids that a woman show what is most beautiful in her.'

She spoke of hiding beauty from the wolves, and I answered jokingly that I was such a creature. I asked her if she had ever loved anybody. Several men had proposed to her, she replied, but she would accept only the hand of someone she loved. Such feelings, though, had not yet entered her realm of experience. We could not have been up there for more than five minutes before she rushed downstairs, I following her, taking care not to stumble in the darkness.

She introduced me to her mother, a shy and gentle woman who was then entertaining guests, one of whom asked me many questions about poetry, such as what makes one begin to write a poem. All I could tell him was that for me no two poems ever came from the same place—if they did, I would be able to write far more. Later, as Azadeh and her brother drove me back to my hotel, she told me her mother had asked her to invite me to dinner the following day.

THE NEXT MORNING I went looking for nomads in the Zagros Mountains around Shiraz. I had a driver, Amoo, who a couple of days before had taken me to Persepolis and the tomb of Cyrus. I wanted nomads, I told him, lots of them. Amoo laughed, saying that among them were bandits who regularly stopped cars and invited their occupants to divest themselves of their excess baggage, and that we might be able to meet some of those. I wasn't sure how serious he was. I mentioned the Qashghais in particular, a Turkic nomadic people, a number of whom I had met some days before, living in the shadow of the Ateshkadé-yé Ardeshir Fire Temple not far from Firuz Abad. I described to Amoo how, in front of her husband, one of the women had danced for me. Amoo told me there was no law in the country that could contain these people, that they were truly free in spirit. These 'nomads' were semi-permanent residents, however, and I wanted now to meet those on their winter journey to the southern provinces. The ones around Firuz Abad, Amoo told me, had already made their way south to Bushehr but we might be able to find a few stragglers.

'A month earlier you could have had all the nomads you like.'

Amoo stopped at a roadside stall to buy some *kashk*, hardened balls of heavily salted yoghurt, which the nomads made and sold en route. This, presumably, was the beginning of my 'nomadic experience'. We drove and drove, speaking of many things, including love and death, which the beautiful mountain scenery seemed to put into perspective. A friend of his, Amoo told me, had just been diagnosed with cancer and had but a month to live. All night Amoo had lain awake, remembering their shared childhood experiences. What would become now of his wife and children? There was no insurance for widows in this country, he told me, which was why so many of them turned to prostitution. The Islamic Revolution and the war with Iraq had made widows of tens of thousands of wives, nearly all of whom were destitute.

'Once I was at a party where my friends had hired a prostitute for the evening. I paid for her to be allowed to go home. My younger brother died at the front, for no good reason. I said to my friends she could have been his wife. She could have been any one of our daughters.'

We spoke also of the legal code, in particular the rarely mentioned stoning of adulterous women, who are first buried to their waists and then pelted to death with small stones. Amoo assured me that this was a barbaric custom originating in the harsh conditions of the desert hundreds of years ago and that it bore no relation to true Islam. More disturbingly, he said it would have been stopped long ago had it not been supported by women, who, despite their powerful calls for political change, did their utmost to preserve the ancient traditions.

'We need another prophet to come,' he said bitterly, 'in order to put right the mistakes we have made in interpreting the wishes of the last one.'

After a couple of hours, Amoo spotted some sheep up in the mountains.

'Where there are sheep,' he said, 'there are nomads, maybe.'

We stopped the car and scrambled from boulder to boulder, poor Amoo stopping every couple of minutes to check his heart rate. Then he shouted to see if there was anyone up there. A youth suddenly appeared from behind some bushes, wearing blue jeans and a jazzy shirt, considerably more surprised to see us than we were to see him.

'What are you doing here?!' he exclaimed.

Amoo translated for me, then looked at me pleadingly as I fumbled for questions. Before I could come up with one, the boy asked me, 'Where are you from?' Amoo told him I had come all the way from England. The boy stared at me as if I were seriously lost.

'I have never met anyone from England in these mountains before.'

There was an awkward silence.

'Do you have any questions you'd like to ask him?' asked Amoo.

'I don't know. I mean, I can't very well ask him if he is a nomad, can I? Or what it feels like to be one?'

'But you did say you wanted to meet some. Look, we've found one, probably the *only* one we'll find today.'

Amoo offered him some *kashk*, which the boy stared at with no great enthusiasm. Clearly he took me for a complete idiot, and there, perched on a stone, sheep bleating all around me, I did rather feel like one.

'No, I've no questions.'

The driver told the boy I was pleased to make his acquaintance, may Allah preserve him. The boy shrugged his shoulders, surely grateful to be living a sane existence. He shouted to his sheep, the sheep moved, and Amoo and I made our way back to Shiraz, speaking of many things indeed but no longer of nomads and their curious lives.

AZADEH'S BROTHER DROVE US to a teagarden on the outskirts of Shiraz where we smoked a water pipe. I found Azadeh much withdrawn. When I asked her if she was all right, she replied, 'I am a person of the night.' Into my lap fell a yellow leaf, which I then presented to her. She recoiled in horror.

'Do you hate me?' she cried. 'This is what giving someone a yellow leaf signifies.'

I apologised profusely, marvelling at my ability to produce *faux pas*.

When we got back into the car she sang another song. 'It is for you,' she said quietly. When I asked what the words meant, she told me it was a song of spiritual love. I remembered what an Arab friend once told me, that in Islamic culture the concept of *wedad*, or spiritual love, is perfectly acceptable within the strict codes governing romance. When we stopped so I could buy flowers for her mother, she followed me into the florist's, ostensibly to help me make the purchase.

'I will never forget you,' she whispered to me. She then said, covering her seriousness with a laugh, 'Your wife would kill you, and then she would kill me too, but then I could love you in Paradise.'

When we got back into the car she took my hand in hers and held it tightly all the way to her house. Once inside, Azadeh disappeared for a while, coming back with a *manghal* (a sort of thurible) that held three or four smoking coals. 'It's a surprise,' she said. She rotated it around my head three times, saying, 'May God protect you from all jealousies.' She then gave me seeds of rue to crumble over the burning coals, asking me to smell the smoke their burning produced. This, I learned, was in order to avert the Evil Eye. Yet again Zoroaster was making his presence felt.

After a magnificent dinner Azadeh took down from her shelf a volume of Hafez's poems and, pressing it between her hands, invited me to sit opposite her. 'You see,' she said, 'I believe what Hafez tells me and sometimes I consult him in order to realise my wishes. We call this *fal* and there are precise rules as to how this should be done. The book must be held upright between the hands like this, and then you run your fingernail across its top edge, finding a place. Wherever the book is opened you must read the poem on the right-hand page, even if it begins on the previous page. I will ask him now to tell me about you.'

Azadeh took a deep breath, closed her eyes and when she opened them began to read a poem she called "The Gardener", which she paraphrased for me. I have since looked for a translation of this poem but without success.

'Hafez compares you to a white flower and welcomes you to his city, saying that although your journey has been a difficult one it is here that you'll find an answer to whatever troubles your mind. He says he trusts you. Also, in your search for God, he says it is not important what your religion is as long as you work hard for that which is most difficult to attain. You will then catch what you desire and watch it rise.'

Azadeh seemed to attach much significance to the fact that my religion didn't matter. We repeated the exercise, this time with me asking about her. The verse we hit upon, which I am not able fully to paraphrase, contained the message that one must not ask what is in the heart for there is too much there to be able to control. As Azadeh translated the poem, tears welled up in her eyes. She then kissed the book, returned it to its place on the shelf, and disappeared into her room. She returned a few minutes later with what she described as her most precious possession, a calligraphy made of one of Hafez's poems, her very favourite. I tried to refuse many times, but she said I must have it.

'In this poem Hafez says, "If you want to know about my heart, there are so many things in it that if I named them all it would be lost. It is better that you don't know about them; otherwise my tongue would not allow me to speak. It is better that you do not sit next to me, and that you do not think about what is in my heart. You are what I came here for."'

All this took place in the presence of her family, but as though inside a bubble. The rest of the afternoon was a kind of surreal prose. Azadeh's aunt and uncle had arrived from the south, bringing with them, in four plastic bags, a whole butchered sheep, and now they sat in the middle of the floor, cleavers in hand, chopping the sheep into smaller and smaller pieces.

I WAS WALKING THROUGH a fairly impoverished area near the main bazaar when a balding, bearded man standing in the doorway of his house beckoned me inside. At first he seemed elderly, and there were running sores all over his face. There wasn't time for me to decline his invitation, for already I was being ushered past a number of women and children. We sat down in an almost bare room with a couple of Qur'anic inscriptions taped to the wall, a few books, and, most incongruously, hanging from a small hook on the door, a pair of boxing gloves. A startlingly pretty girl of about five or six sat down beside me and fixed her gaze on me for the most extraordinary length of time, just occasionally allowing a smile. I was then made to understand that she was this man's daughter. Clearly he was not nearly as old as I had at first thought. I saw through the haggard features and running sores a man my own age, perhaps younger even. After a while, he managed to convey to me that they were Afghan refugees.

A few minutes later his son arrived, Massoud, a boy of eighteen, who was able to speak some English. His father had sent for him to be brought from the market in order to act as interpreter. Massoud had not been to school for three years but such English as he remembered he used with striking eloquence. I can't recall a single problem of communication during the whole of our conversation. Massoud told me his father had been a university professor in Kabul, where he and his family had had a relatively comfortable life. When the Taliban came to power he was ordered to submit to their rules. This was something he would never do, he told them, for he wanted democracy for his country. The Taliban officials went away, saying they would give him a day to reconsider his foolish response. Here Massoud's father, divining our conversation, broke in, and spoke critically of religion, asking why there couldn't be a single faith that drew the best from all beliefs. The family fled Kabul immediately, leaving behind all their property, their house, and their library. Almost all their savings had gone towards bribing people to smuggle them across the border into Iran and now they were in much reduced circumstances. Massoud then showed me the one treasure he'd managed to bring with him from Kabul, his English exercise books. I leafed through the pages, seeing at once that here was a student who got consistently high grades.

'What would you have done had you been able to remain in Kabul?'

'The thing I wanted most of all was to become a doctor. I wanted to travel to England and study there. We are not able to go to school here. The only education I and my brothers and sisters get now are the lessons our father teaches us every evening. You see, though, how he is.'

The father, because of whatever was now tearing at his proud frame, could not work anymore, and Massoud and his younger brother supported the whole family. Together, they brought in approximately three dollars a day. The boys sold old clothes on the street. Being Afghan refugees, they could not get a place in the bazaar itself. When I asked Massoud about his future, he said it was without hope. They had no legal rights, no citizenship or security of any kind and a single error, a single scrape with the law, could result in their being sent back to Afghanistan where they would face almost certain death.

'Such hopes as I have,' he told me, 'are snakes in the grass.'

I could barely believe my ears, that he had somehow remembered this sentence, which no longer seemed hackneyed but, on the contrary, deeply profound.

'This is my one escape,' Massoud said, pointing to the boxing gloves. 'I love to box, but also I need to be able to protect myself when people try to rob me. A few months ago, some Iranian boys beat me up and took the little money I had made that day. We suffer much abuse here.'

We were brought nan stuffed with potatoes and then cakes, which I am sure the mother had rushed out to buy. Later, when his father left the room, I pressed upon Massoud twenty dollars, which was probably the most money he had seen for a while, certainly enough to pay half the month's rent of 300,000 rials. With confusion and tears in his eyes, he said it would be the worst thing in the world for him to accept money for hospitality—this would be to go against his religion. Eventually I managed to persuade him that the money had nothing to do with his family's hospitality, that it was meant as a gift and as such did not really belong to this particular time frame. Finally he accepted, but only when I pushed the money beneath the cushion so that he would not have to touch it. When I left, Massoud gave me his address, and when I looked at it I was startled to see it was not in Shiraz but in Kabul.

'That is our home,' he said, 'and perhaps one day we will be able to return.'

His father, who had just come back, bowed his head in silence.

'Will the world help us do so?' he asked.

A PHOTOGRAPH TAKEN of Azadeh and me, in the tea garden where I offered her the yellow leaf, has an odd shadowy bar running down its middle, separating us. I can think of no physical explanation for it, and am tempted to read into this the division that sometimes comes between people of different cultures, but then I wonder if it were not symbolic of still darker forces that separate people.

My penultimate meeting with Azadeh, which began tenderly enough, by the end of the evening made my blood freeze. We went back to her family's home, where, together with her two brothers, we got into a four-cornered row over Islam. Oddly enough, I found myself mediating between her and her brothers, the youngest of whom scorned religion, and shouted at her, calling her a primitive, adding bitterly that she deserved to go into a harem. I had to admire Azadeh's eloquence, and her coolness in withstanding the verbal assault of her brothers. When it came to divine law (*al-shari'ah*) and, in particular, the stoning of women she was resolute. I remembered Amoo telling me that it was women especially who insisted on upholding retributive justice. I wished then the question had never been raised.

'A woman being stoned to death,' I argued, 'is this what God desires?'

'The stones chosen are of about this size,' Azadeh said, indicating one about the size of a plum.

'Suppose, then, Muslims are right and Christ is *not* the son of God—'

'We *are* right. We respect him as one of the greatest of the prophets.'

'What, then, is one to make of that revolutionary statement, "He that is without sin among you, let him first cast a stone at her." Would you argue with the words of a prophet?'

'Show me that passage in the Qur'an.'

'It's in the Holy Bible.'

'So, *not* in Qur'an then?'

I was feeling depressed that a woman of such tenderness, with such a fine measure of human nature, could put all that was best in her to the service of something so unspeakable. For Azadeh, though, religion was not a system devised by man in order to praise God but the word of God himself. There could be no arguing with her on this score. Or could there? The words in the Qur'an are open to interpretation, and highly educated Muslims had told me that the stoning of an adulterous woman is sanctioned only when there are four witnesses to the sexual act, which was unlikely. Azadeh was not prepared to budge on the issue. Would she cast the first stone?

'THIS IS A *SADLY* DAY,' Azadeh said. 'Please come back soon.'

She was silent for most of the drive to the airport. All the bitterness of the night before had begun to evaporate. I presented her with Dostoevsky's *The Brothers Karamazov* in Persian. It would have been *Crime and Punishment* had I been able to find a copy. As I slipped back into my earlier affection for her, I realised that I'd found in Shiraz what I didn't know I'd come looking for, a cleansing of a mind that, in recent months, had become thick with anger, impotence, and grime. I had been suffering a crisis of faith, and Azadeh led me back to a belief in the efficacy of poetry. I told her this, adding that *she* was what Hafez said I had come looking for.

'Yes,' she answered, 'and now you must follow God.'

When it came time to say our farewells, I touched the side of her face, just the once. A friendly kiss was not permissible.

Toronto'd

ON THE TRAIN FROM MONTREAL to Toronto I fell into conversation with a lawyer who told me that he had just recently fallen in love for the first time. This would seem a bit late for a man in his mid fifties and also, because I'm given to reserve, it struck me as premature of him to have dropped such a nugget into the first five minutes of an acquaintance. I am, however, the deadly carrier of a thousand secrets, most of them entrusted to me by people I meet but once. I must have some kind of face. The lawyer wore a patterned shirt with wide sleeves. I wondered about the ex-wife he mentioned some minutes later, whether he had ever been in love with her. Stendhal has much to say about love's illusions, whereas this man merely winced, as if he had bitten through a wormed apple. Why was I going to Toronto, he asked me. I said I was giving a poetry reading there. 'Well, well,' he said, 'I just wrote a poem, my first ever, which I gave to Anne.' (Anne is not, of course, her real name.) Anne then showed it to her best friend, Susie, a move that, in the lawyer's mind, raised some question as to whether a poem could be allowed to enter the public domain without infringing intellectual copyright. I urged him not to sue, explaining that he had just doubled his readership, which was more than I had done. Anyway, he told me, it was now incumbent on him to produce a second poem.

He had been experimenting on and off with haiku, finding it tougher than he expected to squeeze so much of his newly found love into a mere seventeen syllables. I suggested he try limericks.

We spoke for five and a half hours, covering much of the world, and, in particular, a part of it I hadn't given much thought to for some time. Doubtless the pines I saw from the train window pricked old memories alive. I grew up in country such as this, which not even England's 'dark satanic mills' can fully erase. And it might well have been the leathery glint of a crow as it rose above muddy fields that put Chico in mind, Chico who I used to observe in a small greasy spoon in Ottawa in 1969, Chico, leader of the Satan's Choice, a motorcycle gang not quite as notorious as the Hell's Angels but demonic enough all the same. When one of their number died, his fellows, as a mark of respect, would piss into his open grave. I saw Chico in battle once, against a pretender to his throne, and I marvelled at the ritualistic beauty of the encounter. Chico won. Chico was now, so the lawyer informed me, the subject of biker literature. I hadn't thought about Chico for at least three decades. It was at this point I looked out the train window and saw the factory where my father worked for many years, all of them in bitterness, for although he had trained as a naval officer history pushed him down another route. What was doubly painful for him is that he could see, from the high tower where he was, the ships as they sailed down the Saint Lawrence.

We spoke, the lawyer and I, of many other matters and, in truth, I took him for a likeable enough figure. We discussed London, Paris and Rome and their respective cuisines. And he'd been to Russia too. We discussed politics, in which matter he clearly was to the Right of me, I who am to the Right of so many people. Such is my contrary nature, though, that the more we spoke the more to the Left I began to slide. I became the Pinko to his Tory blue. We discussed books although he was poor at remembering authors and titles, which made me suspect he might have been bluffing a little. Also we covered the rocky terrain of justice, he telling me of his impressions of the American penal system, and, as if on cue, one of the penitentiaries dotted about this part of Ontario grew in the distance. Several kids I knew from school were sent there so that they might perfect their criminality although few of them became so accomplished as to avoid a second or third sentence. A surprising number of them died in car crashes. Some went into business management while still others, Kenny S—, for example, never went anywhere at all. The police always knew where to look for Kenny because no sooner did he steal a car than he drove it straight home. They found him once, driving the car in circles in a field behind his parent's house. The penitentiary was quite large but, the lawyer told me, it was nothing as compared to America where such places often cover a few square miles. Many of the inmates had been wrongly imprisoned for mere trifles, he said, while others, the really hard cases, were beyond any possibility of redemption. They don't even know what *bad* is and as such there is little justification for their existence. I didn't ask whether he spoke ironically or if this was a view he shared.

An hour or so later, the train stopped at Trenton. I wondered if Pepsi were still alive. A native of that town, Pepsi would get drunk on Pepsi, there being some mysterious agent in that substance that prompted him to sing, which he could not do when sober, in a voice remarkably like Frank Sinatra's, and indeed had nature given him a better, more presentable, face he might have made a name for himself on the nightclub circuit as a Sinatra impersonator. The last time I saw him he was slumped over a parking meter, singing "Strangers in the Night", so convincingly one could just about hear the Nelson Riddle strings behind his marooned voice.

As the train entered the first of Toronto's many satellite towns the lawyer told me that if I were in a room of twenty people and there was a psychopath among them I would not be able to say which one he was, except perhaps he might be the most charming, humorous and gentle. As we came into Union Station he asked me where I was going and when I told him Gerrard Street East where I'd be staying at the house of another lawyer and his wife, he said he'd be passing that way by taxi and that he'd drop me. As we walked away from the train two girls passed us.

'Hey, you there,' he blared.

The girls stopped.

'Get out of my way, will you.'

When we reached the entrance to the station he paused to smoke a cigarillo, standing stiffly as if priming himself for battle, and then hailed a cab driven by a man of Asiatic appearance. When the driver began to spout ordinary pleasantries, the lawyer cut him off, saying we were not tourists and that he was not to waste time.

'Green light,' he shouted, 'C'mon, *move!*'

The driver turned around.

'You know what you are, *you*, *you*, you are an ignorant man. You are stupid, this I can see. I know more than you ever will.'

The lawyer smirked. Quite impressed by his brisk defence, I asked the driver where he was from.

'Iran,' he replied.

We spoke of the places I'd been to and of Hafez and Persian classical music. The driver drove more and more slowly, much to the lawyer's annoyance, and then he put on a tape of the recently deceased poet, Ahmad Shamloo. Only a couple of days before, in Montreal, the poet Eric Ormsby told me he had known Shamloo when they were together at Princeton. It was the first time I had heard him mentioned outside Iran but then for Ormsby the world's a village. My friend described him as 'short and quite compact with a leonine head of white hair.' When I visited Iran, Shamloo was the poet of whom everyone spoke. A man I met in Isfahan wept when he told me of his death and described to me how, in his final moments, Shamloo asked for pen and paper and wrote his farewell poem. Shamloo's images slipped through the censor's net although it could well be, in a country where only poetry is bigger than politics or religion, the censor himself made the holes extra large. And now here, in a taxi in Toronto, was Shamloo's dark and mellifluous voice.

The greater part of any impression of a city is made within the first few minutes of being there. One may get to love or even hate a place, but that initial taste, whether sweet or bitter, is difficult to remove. The German for 'death' is *tod*, which is perhaps rather too laborious a pun for the title of this piece, although one may think of being *towed* along by black-plumed horses, in a funeral cortège. *Toro* is, of course, the Spanish for bull and one thinks of the hush of the spectators before the toreador sinks his blade. Actually 'Toronto' is of Aboriginal origin, meaning 'a place of meeting', where the different tribes would congregate. One thinks of Toronto now as a place from where people disperse, for I am reliably informed there are few original Torontonians left. Where could they have all gone? (Where, for that matter, have all the Londoners gone? Actually I was soon to learn the fate of one.) My somewhat forced title grew out of a feeling for what Toronto, city as *verb*, does to me. It is surprising how many people, even the most patriotic Canadians, equate Toronto with spiritual death or speak of a city striving to be something else, New York, for instance. There are even those who can barely contain their feelings of antipathy towards the place. Montrealers are particularly hostile.

I have no desire, of course, to be rude about a city that apparently a great number of people love. And where, in fact, I was subjected to several kindnesses. Margaret Atwood, who can afford to go anywhere, still lives there. David Mason, an antiquarian bookseller of considerable repute, appears happy enough to live there. My friend Bill Blissett, scholar extraordinaire and friend of David Jones, whose memory he has preserved in a marvellous book called *The Long Conversation*, would not, I believe, willingly choose to live anywhere else. Wyndham Lewis, on the other hand, called the place 'a sanctimonious icebox' and out of his experience of living there came his novel *Self Condemned*, which many admirers, Cy Fox among them, consider his most personal and bitter and accurate. Cy too lives in Toronto, but would be only too happy to leave.

I had been to Toronto many years before, in 1969, so I was coming to it anew, with only a dim memory I could barely substantiate. Ah yes, now I remember. A wispy-bearded Mongolian giant on Bloor Street demanded money of me, which I gave, and then I slipped into a café in Yorkville, when Yorkville was *really* Yorkville, the hippest of places, where a girl with flaking mascara about her eyes offered to read me my fortune, which she did, which was so terrible I fled the city right there and then. I am morbidly sensitive. My impression of the city now is that many people there seem to put on a second pair of teeth, a metal substitute of some kind but pearly white in appearance. Quite unreasonably, perhaps, I place the burden of these feelings upon the broad shoulders of the lawyer who underwent the werewolf-like transformation the city seemed to demand of him, and who stared at me in sheer disbelief when the cabdriver shook my hand goodbye, the green numbers of the fare on his meter increasing all the time.

WHEN I ENTERED the darkened auditorium at the Harbourfront Centre, where my reading was to take place, I noticed a man sitting alone at one of the round tables, a faint smile on his face. I thought he looked familiar and I thought so again when I spotted him from the stage, still wearing that faint smile. After the reading he came up to me, and then I remembered immediately who he was. I shall reveal his identity here only by the magnolia tree that flowers in front of his house. I think he may still be a fugitive. 'Magnolia' was one of the very first people my wife and I got to know in London, when we were living in Earls Court Square. There was about him the seraphic quality a certain type of Englishman has, which, with the slightest turning of a dial, turns him from a collector of postage stamps into a fearsome warrior, a perfumed builder of empires. The seemingly fey is merely a sheath concealing the sharpest of blades. (The physical breed of whom I speak is becoming increasingly scarce, which makes me suspect there is a connection between physiognomy and the spirit of the times.) We had both gone to Poetry Round, a group of mainly psychotics posing as a literary circle. I read my bad poems and Magnolia read his rather better ones. Also, we went to the nearby Troubadour Coffeehouse, where the Monday night readings were run under the auspices of a man so proletarian in his thinking he went only by the name of Dave, which alone served to indicate he had come from a background of some privilege. Apparently time has been gentler to Magnolia than it has been to me, for while I was certain it was him he was not so sure it was me.

'Ah,' I said, 'whatever became of that business with the plumbing?'

The first thing that flew into my thoughts was a mystery I had never been able to solve, and which I felt had to do with Magnolia's sudden disappearance from our lives almost thirty years before. My old friend had got himself a job on a building site, posing as a plumber, complete with tools which he especially purchased for that purpose, and when, a month or so later, the water ran backwards through the pipes, the toilet bowls overflowed and fresh leaks sprung everywhere he fled London. I do remember questioning his sense of morality and my opinion is that he was somewhat chastened by the experience. All these years later, Magnolia searched his memory and was surprised that I had recalled what he himself had consigned to oblivion.

'Goodness me,' he said, 'you remember that! I had quite forgotten.'

I guided him towards my wife several yards away.

'Do you remember — ?'

'Oh,' she cried, 'the plumber!'

Magnolia, the blondest Englishman ever to have been born beneath blue skies, when he arrived in Canada launched himself on a fresh career, masquerading, in print only, as a black journalist for a black community newspaper. Articles appeared under the name of 'James Mondo', but this is a further chapter in his life that may have to be gone into elsewhere. I am not sure he would welcome the exposure. Should he be thought here a perennial rogue he is, in truth, the gentlest of gentlemen. Any accidents of fortune are his alone. As of late he has been the publisher of books of a technological and environmental nature, including the evocatively titled *Storage Tanks in Ontario*, whose pages I have yet to peruse. Also I have heard that a favourite goldfish of his has met a rather sad demise. It was, in his words, 'apparently pronged on the ends of a racoon's almost mandarin fingernails.' There remains, despite his many years in Canada, much velvet in Magnolia's style.

ON THE SAME TRAIN, going back to Montreal, I sat beside a young woman, a university student with a moonlike face and dark eyes, who, I learned later, was Persian. This was after I asked her if she were Italian. Such memories as came to the fore on the outward journey were now, on the homeward, tucked safely back inside. I was solidly in the present tense. When, almost exactly halfway to Montreal, suddenly I sneezed the lady beside me said, in the faintest of voices, 'Bless you,' which were her first words to me. She later confessed to being a touch nervous about the SARS virus, which had elected Toronto as its North American incubation centre. 'Are you Italian?' I asked her. I have a deep fascination for where people come from, especially if I think they are of a certain tribe, but my enquiries in that direction have led one or two people to suspect me of being rude. The girl beside me seemed happy enough to be asked about her origins but then perhaps she was being excessively polite.

Azadeh had never heard of Ahmad Shamloo although she did say her parents consulted the *divan* of Hafez as one might a horoscope. This is the practice of *fal*, which involves holding a volume of Hafez's poems upright between one's hands and then, after asking a question touching upon any matter central to one's life, whether it be business or love, running one's fingernail across the top edge of the book, seeking a place. Wherever the book is opened one must begin immediately to read the poem on the right hand page even if it begins on the previous page. Somewhere in those lines, if one reads deeply enough, Hafez offers sound advice. Azadeh was going to visit Iran soon and felt shame at knowing so little about the country from whence she came. She had not even heard of the Zoroastrians and so I informed her that she might originally have been one, in another life that is. She was appalled by what I told her about the vultures picking over the bones of the newly dead. She warmed, on the other hand, to the idea of an eternal flame. I noticed she had two fingers wrapped together in a single bandage and also, well before she first spoke, that she was reading *The Encyclopaedia of Serial Killers*. She was highlighting a number of passages in ultramarine.

'You seem far too gentle,' I said, 'to be reading such a tome.'

Why did I put on such a musty voice?

'One day I hope to work for the FBI, creating criminal profiles,' she replied, 'and besides, it's one of my favourite books.'

An adoring boyfriend had given it to her, for her 21st birthday, inscribed 'to "Ozzie" with X's and O's'.

'Go to *N*,' I told her.

She turned the pages.

'Keep going,' I said. 'Stop.'

I informed her that I had the dubious pleasure once of holding in my hands Denis Nilsen's notebook in which he blandly recorded his meetings with, and his subsequent dismemberment of, a number of young men. After reading a page or two, I could proceed no further and still I'm not sure if it was for want of a decent prose style. Would I have probed further had the author managed to scintillate? Why are psychopaths so often bores? I should think they torture the flesh because they have insufficient imagination with which to reach even the simplest truths inside people. Also, I had handled the pots and pans in which Nilsen cooked certain body parts of his victims. (I am not at liberty to say where this took place.) Azadeh was impressed that I should have come so close to what she could study only at a distance. She was, I emphasise, extremely gentle. As we approached Montreal I told her a lawyer had recently told me one could sit in a room of twenty people and never know which one of them was the psychopath, except that he might be the jolliest one there.

One Night in Marseilles

I FELL INTO CONVERSATION WITH A Moroccan prostitute. Actually it was not so much conversation as playful banter, a constructed space where one's demons may dance for a while. I was probably wasting a busy girl's time. She asked me where I came from and what I did and I told her I sold books, *livres anciens*, and she laughed to think one could survive by means of such trifles. What was I doing in Marseilles talking to a prostitute about the antiquarian book trade? I asked her if business was good and she pulled a clownish face. We both had been spiked by the video trade. She worked out of one of the dingier bars close to the train station, which was empty save for her two bored female colleagues and a single barman who looked as though his dog had just died of rabies. She was not like the women at the so-called 'American bars' (Russian in reality) down at the harbour front, all coiffure and cleavage. She was dressed sloppily enough, sweater and jeans, as if for home. She lifted her sweater a little to show me a slightly flabby belly, almost as if to indicate she was at the lower end of the flesh trade, and laughed when we said goodbye. A fool I may be, but she haunted me for the whole of that evening and she haunts me still, if only just a little.

I'm beginning to get her features in a scramble. What is it about the human face that it should be the most memorable thing in existence and yet its atoms are the quickest to disperse? There are those whom I have known at length, who, although I saw them from a thousand angles, come back to me in only the merest of glimpses and always in the same few frames. What survives of my Moroccan is a downward curve in her smile, and, beneath the pockmarks, a prettiness of a kind that made me hesitate. '*Vous êtes très jolie,*' I said, after refusing her advances. The words played back to me, in the space of this prose, make me queasy—but they were, at the time, for better or worse, truly meant. I would like to believe my utterance, silly though it was, freed us from the burden of commerce. There was a discernible shift of tone. Sex off the agenda, we jabbered a while. I did not ask her any of the questions I should most like to have had answers to. What, for example, were the circumstances in her life that she should have allowed herself to be cut off from her family and culture? After all, an Arab girl in her position would be unlikely to find a way home. I wonder, though, how truthful I've been here. I might rescue her in my fantasies, but I'd also violate those very aspects of her I want saved.

AMONG LITERARY EXERCISES there are few more doubtful than those written by men about prostitutes, where the tendency is to fall between sentiment and prurience. Why admit these kerb crawlers of the intellect other than to get 'on the cheap' a spectacle of one's own innate badness or goodness? Whatever way one looks at it, it is an unhealthy play of the intellect, a mere preening of the mind. There are those, Dostoevsky, for example, and perhaps, in terms of sympathy, I should count myself among them, who find their God only in the lowliest of places. Surely I build her up, my Moroccan, for my own purposes. Shall I now make her my patron saint of Marseilles? A single cackle from her direction will bring down the edifice I make of her sad and miserable existence.

What made me go to Marseilles in the first place? I had been with friends in the Cevennes. After so much postcard loveliness perhaps I was hungry for a filmic atmosphere, which, like Alain Delon, was both sinister and edged with finesse. Alone among countries, France is the multiplier of whatever mood one takes there: if one goes there with a feeling of joy one will be rewarded tenfold, but heaven forbid should one go there in low spirits for one leaves feeling considerably worse than before. Paris is a particularly dangerous place to be but the same holds for the rest of France, even if not quite to the same degree. I have tried this theory out on friends and have yet to be disabused of it. I had gone to the Cevennes after a major disappointment and although I supped well and conversed at length I did not find a panacea. I went to Marseilles to feed my silences. I spent a couple of hours walking before I found, and had to pay for, a double room, a miserable hole of a place that seemed to smell of every person who had ever stayed there. I opened the shutters wide and still the air would not move. I then wandered all over the city, enjoying only the Arab quarter, its sounds and smells. On the whole, I did not much care for the place.

I've been reading Robert Louis Stevenson's essay, *On the Enjoyment of Unpleasant Places* (1874). 'We see places through our humours as through differently coloured glasses,' he writes. 'We are ourselves a term in the equation, a note of the chord, and make discord or harmony almost at will … And even where there is no harmony to be elicited by the quickest and most obedient of spirits, we may still embellish a place with some attraction of romance.' Stevenson is most definitely one of *my* people in that he is a corrective to my own morbid tendencies. Of all the writers with whom I'd most like to have a drink, it's R.L.S. What friends we might have become. When I was in the Cevennes, I read (of course) Stevenson's *Travels with a Donkey*—also Joseph Roth's *The String of Pearls*, which is about a Viennese prostitute who is called upon to act as a double for a countess spotted at a ball by the visiting Shah of Persia. The easily duped Shah rewards her with a string of pearls, the sale of which precipitates a whole series of tragedies. We may see in this, if we look hard enough, an anticipation of the fall of the Habsburg Empire.

A couple of days ago, I was relating all this to a friend of mine, the poet and translator, Jennie Feldman, and no sooner did I mention Marseilles than she exclaimed, 'Oh, I just *love* Marseilles!' She had lived there for a year. She began a small revolution in my thoughts, which, together with Stevenson's essay, produced a ray powerful enough to cut through the murkiness gathered there, even if it did take some days for its light to reach me. There is, indeed, something about Marseilles.

After I spoke to the Moroccan I went back to my hotel, exhausted from not having slept the night before. I should think I had not slept out of anticipation of going *to* Marseilles and now I could not sleep because I was *in* Marseilles. A few minutes after I settled into the bed whose mattress was higher on one side than the other, which made me feel as though I might at any moment spill onto the floor, I felt an all too familiar burning sensation. I have just checked my eleventh edition of the *Encyclopædia Britannica*. The Latin name for the bed bug is *Cimex lectularius*. The more familiar English word is derived from the Celtic *bwg* meaning 'ghost' or 'goblin', for such was the terror its attacks at first inspired. I am rather surprised to learn that in England, until about three centuries ago, the bed bug made only a rare appearance. I am sorry to learn that human blood is the sole food of this species. That night in Marseilles they induced in me not so much terror as a sense of weariness brought on by the realisation that I'd been here too many times before. Such have been the choices I made in life that I have been forced to economise. Too often I have found myself on sunken beds in hot countries. And here, where I had paid for a double, whole continents of bites began to rise on my flesh. I moved across the room to a second bed where a mosquito (I think it was just the one) dived at me in the darkness. I put the light on several times but against the several peeling layers of floral wallpaper—a domestic archaeology was to be found here—it was too well camouflaged. All through the night I listened to the sound of police sirens, which suggested that perhaps Marseilles was living up to its reputation for violence. There's almost always trouble when the air doesn't move. A woman moaned rhythmically from one of the windows opposite. Suddenly her cries of ecstasy were cut into, displaced by a wild laughter of seagulls. It was as if some sound technician in his lab had perfectly spliced the two sounds together.

At four o'clock in the morning, fed up with Marseilles, fed up with the bites, fed up with the mosquitoes, I packed my bag and walked though unlit streets to the train station, going past the bar where the Moroccan prostitute had been. A metal blind had been pulled down. I took the five o'clock train to Nice where, that following night, during the course of an electrical storm, a bolt of lightning struck and destroyed the noisy generator just outside my hotel window, which had been keeping me awake. I welcomed the silence. I tossed and turned some more. France was indeed the multiplier of what one takes there, and in my disquietude I wondered whether Allah had room in his paradise for a Moroccan girl who'd been cast adrift.

A Journey to the Sun's Grave

W HAT IS IT ABOUT ISLANDS that when one asks how to get somewhere the directions one receives are close to incomprehensible? I tested this idea out on a very tall Finn in Tallinn and he agreed, saying, 'Yes, ask someone on a *very* small island the way to the sea and he'll look around him like this,' and here I must ask the reader to imagine the facial expression, somewhere between mischief and deep foolishness, which he reproduced for me. I was on the relatively large Estonian island of Saaremaa, more specifically, in the inland village of Karja, when I asked a shy, plump, young woman the way to the mediaeval church of the same name. She seemed aghast at the boldness of my question. 'Over there,' she replied, seemingly wanting to get shot of me, her arm covering an arc of roughly 45 degrees. All I could see on the churchless horizon was a massive barn, the largest I have ever seen, a tumbledown relic of Soviet collectivisation, a ghost barn, misty white light showing through where the planks had been torn away, newly put to private uses. Soon enough, nothing of it will remain except, perhaps, its immense concrete floor, a puzzle for archaeologists in the future. This mammoth ruin had been an article of faith in an idea that was adhered to for only half a century; I was seeking a more permanent structure.

After walking another four kilometres, stopping midway at the wooden Angla windmills, most haunting when seen in morning fog, I finally found it, Saaremaa's oldest and loveliest church, dedicated to St. Catherine (Katariina). A magical church, small on the outside it seems large when one steps inside. There are mathematical reasons for this, which have to do with the vault being twice the height the walls, and which gives the soul cause to move, swallow-like, beyond its mortal frame. I had been advised to take note of the magical symbols on the ceiling above the altar, among them a triskelion, a swastika-like figure comprising three legs bent at the knees, eternally running, so it seems, in its own space.

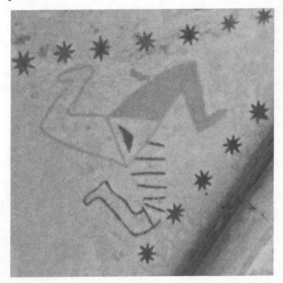

This curious symbol which is found in many countries is, in these northerly latitudes, emblematic both of the Nordic god Odin and the Holy Trinity, and bespeaks a meeting of pagan and Christian, Christianity on this isle being only marginally older than the church itself. As well as representing past, present and future, the triskelion is symbolic of the sun.

According to ancient Nordic legend, the sun was buried, only eighteen kilometres away, at Kaali. There are innumerable variants on this legend and one comes from as far away as ancient Greece, with the myth of Phaeton, son of the sun, whose tomb, somewhere in the far north, was said to have resembled an island lake. The witches of ancient Viro, a versatile bunch, were not only capable of plucking the moon out of the skies but also of having hidden away the sun on the iron mountain of an unnamed island. Saaremaa means 'island' and is therefore an island without a name, and it was from there, too, that some of the earliest iron implements come. The Finnish epic poem, the *Kalevala*, has passages referring to a great cataclysmic event there, and in Estonian mythology the hero Kalevipoeg, son of Kalev, on the road to hell, found his journey's end at a small round lake encircled with trees. This last clearly describes the place.

There are many other mythic strands but what they all have in common is the image of a sun hidden or buried. What lies behind this is a real event: Kaali was created by a meteorite, the most recent of any great size to have struck Europe, and, if one accepts the estimates of some scientists, it fell to earth within historical or folk memory, as little as 2,400 years ago. The explosion it made was, in all likelihood, as powerful as Hiroshima, although the destruction was more localised. Small wonder, then, that news of it would have spread over thousands of miles. Small wonder, too, that there would be myths and legends aplenty to accommodate such an incredible event. It is said that Kurasaare, the capital of Saarema, has its linguistic roots in the Nostratic, the hypothetical ancestral language from which many others came, *kura* in Mesopotamian meaning 'lord of the underworld'. The death of the gods, which is how this must have seemed to observers at the time, finds its expression most recently in Wagner's *Götterdammerung*. The old gods die hard in Saaremaa. Pagan belief seems to have insinuated itself even in the most Christian of spaces.

In Tallinn, I met Karl Kello, one of the great experts on Estonian history and mythology, and himself the author of a book on Kaali, *The Pharaoh of the North* (2004). There is nothing of a mythological nature that has not been revealed in this work and it is to Kello I owe my acknowledgements and gratitude. A gentle, retiring figure, he spoke lovingly of the two places.

'It is possible to go there and touch it. It is real. With Karja and Kaali geographically so close, they become a single entity, a symbiosis, with a common history and culture.'

When I asked Kello whether there was any one symbol associated with Kaali that for him took precedence above all the others, he said it was that three-legged symbol of the sun. And looking at it, in Karja church, and remembering this triskelion differed from others in that it has a broken leg, I could not but admire the coherence of his argument. It seems that for Kello all roads lead to Kaali.

SAAREMAA IS ALSO ONE of the candidates for the mythical Ultima Thule. Joanna Kavenna devotes a chapter to it in her book, *The Ice Museum, In Search of the Lost Land of Thule* (2005), in which she interviews the first president of the newly independent Estonia, the late Lennart Meri, who had few doubts on that score. *Tuli*, he said, is Estonian for fire. In his book *Silverwhite*, Meri sought a *mythos* that would enshrine Estonia's independence. The focus, for him, was the crater of Kaali, whose creation had ramifications not just for Estonian but for the whole of Scandinavian and Germanic culture. It was a matter of some irony for him that when the Nazis came to Saaremaa and unleashed their destructive forces, they defiled the very birthplace of Germanic myth.

When the fourth-century BC Greek explorer Pytheus left us his tantalising glimpse of Ultima Thule, which survives only in the writings of others, he spoke of how the barbarians who lived there showed him the place where the sun was put to rest. What makes Saaremaa an attractive candidate is that for Pytheus the apocalyptic event that took place there would have been recent news. The question of *where* Ultima Thule actually is and whether it is Iceland, Greenland, Svalbard or even Britain, is largely a matter of faith, but Saaremaa became for me an agnostic choice.

Somewhat incongruously, the crater of Kaali is reached by walking through a school playground. One passes the white schoolhouse and climbs up a short path of what could be the mound of some old hill fort and from the top of the ridge, surmounted with trees, one looks down into a small round lake of 80 to 120 metres in diameter depending on the season. Quite a few Estonians celebrate their marriages there. There are dark hints that once upon a time it may have been the scene of human sacrifices. And there are those, of course, who sacrifice themselves to marriage. The remains of a stone wall surrounding the lake point to this having been a cult site, and indeed there are powerful traditions of taboo associated with the place, some of which are sexual in origin. The very name 'Kaali', with its hints of a destructive Indian goddess, raises questions almost too complicated to pursue, and the parish in which it is located is called Püha, which means 'taboo'. One such taboo has its echoes in Wagner's Ring Cycle, with the marriage between Siegfried and his sister. The meteorite might well be seen as divine retribution. There are similarly disturbing resonances in the *Kalevala*. One local legend describes how the estate of one who sexually transgressed, again involving the marriage of brother and sister, sank into a hole, which was thereafter filled with water. Curiously, nobody has yet gotten to the bottom of that lake. Kello told me a terrible story of nineteenth-century farmhands who dug there for mud to use as fertiliser in the neighbouring fields and died from the methane gas that was released. Ancient curses sometimes have a physical, even chemical, aspect to them.

The things one goes to see, so often they fail to make sense. The ruins of a Greek temple might make for a nice photograph but without a few words of explanation they will be quite empty of significance. Kaali is even more problematic in that either it can be seen as the most magical of places, which it was for me, and this probably because I was lucky enough to be there alone, or, as the tall Finn in Tallinn told me, it can be seen as nothing more than a hole in the ground. One thing I found proves otherwise. I spotted a strange growth on the trunk of a tree, which, when viewed from a certain angle, looks like a human head, a melancholy god with green hair gazing down at what put paid to his existence. The same legend, paradoxically, helps also to preserve his memory.

It is quite reasonable to suppose that the site of an event so terrible would have so many legends attached to it; it would be curious were this *not* the case. What survives through into the modern age, which sees mostly holes where once there were wondrous tales? I asked Karl Kello if he could summarise for me whether the fact of Kaali can be said to have touched the soul of the Estonian people; he thought for a while, and then said it was a beautiful fairy tale, as all such tales should be, but that when one adds to this the idea of the sky falling to earth, and the darkness that ensues, that the Estonians have adopted a fatalistic 'come what may' attitude towards life. 'The whole of time goes round and round,' he said, and one could see the triskelion's past, present and future turning in his mind's eye, 'and it does not depend on you.' His answer, if one considers the many vicissitudes of Estonian history, was by no means a cursory one.

There is a joke doing the rounds in Tallinn, which has Estonians in stitches. Apparently it helps to know something of the characters at whom it pokes gentle fun. Standing on the rim of the crater are three people: President Lennart Meri, his successor, Arnold Rüütel, and President Rüütel's Minister of Education, Mrs. Mailis Reps, who, for reasons unexplained to me, always raises a chuckle. President Meri, ever mindful of mythic significance, waxes mystically on the ancient event, speaks of the fate that allowed for the meteorite to have landed *here* of all places. President Rüütel says, 'And what a coincidence that it should have fallen into the lake.' 'Yes,' the Minister of Education chimes in, 'And so close to the schoolhouse too.'

The Gardens of Kolymbetra

for Christopher Middleton

1

WOMAN WITH A MEDUSA HEAD of hair sells tickets at the entrance to the *Giardino della Kolymbetra*, the sunken gardens adjacent to, and a hundred steps or so further down from, the Valley of the Temples outside Agrigento. She strikes me as the tutelary spirit of the place, she with her solid grasp of five languages of which, yes, Walloon's the surprise. She was born in Belgium but has returned to what her blood always dictated as home. It is easy to imagine that the small lake constructed here in 480 B.C. to commemorate victory over the Carthaginians at the battle of Himera was actually for *her*. It is only one's wilful ignorance of another person's life that allows for such fancies, of course—the poetical mind prefers ten facts rather than a thousand upon which to build a theme—but she really does seem to have stepped from a black-figure Greek vase. She squeezes fresh orange juice. She does so not as some comforting angel or to drive one to yet deeper reverie but, at a euro a pop, to increase the garden's revenue.

Downwards I go, brushing past broom, *pistacia lentiscus*, tamarisk, terebinth, euphorbia, myrtle, almond and mulberry trees, a scent of orange blossom in the air, the distant hum of a swarm of bees. Empedocles would have known these gardens, Pindar too. The inhabitants of the ancient city of Akragas were much given to pleasure. Plato who visited the city says of them that they built as if they were never to die, and ate as if they had not an hour to live. They drank too. They became flabby over time, and, the tables turned, suffered defeat at the hands of their old enemies. Sicily is an isle of defeats and yet the greater number of them were victories for culture. It's there even in what one sits down to at table. Culture resides not only in broken temples. The artificial lake, which was used as a fish farm, filled up with silt only a century or so after it was made but the fact of those mineral deposits and of the sheltering limestone to one side of the valley makes this place wonderfully conducive to plant growth.

As I descend into these twelve acres of heaven whose existence owes much to the hell of the Carthaginian slaves who constructed the elaborate system of tunnels and aqueducts that feeds the gardens still, and into the citrus grove that contains countless species of orange, mandarin and lemon—some of which are so rare they survive only here—I carry within me not so much the substance as the spirit of Christopher Middleton's poem "The Old Tour Guide—His Interpreter". With its sense of going down, down, down from one level to the next, to where, at the final stage, one is taken by surprise, and by this I mean the *deeper surprise* that is the essence of all art, the poem has been my guide on a number of occasions. A couple of its lines could have been written specifically for this place:

> Let the valley track the turning of your eyes
> And always haunt the here and now you see.

I do what the signs tell me not to and pluck an orange from a tree, its taste just a little bitter, but such its magical transfusion that I swallow down with it whole centuries. The peeling lies bright upon the earth. I feel no guilt over it. Our world will survive this transgression. And looking up a little, above an ancient olive tree, estimated by its girth to be some eight centuries old, I see the somewhat spurious reconstruction of the *Tempio dei Dioscuri* also known as *Tempio di Castore e Polluce* (Castor and Pollux). There is no better vantage point than from where I stand for it's as if those three columns together are the skeleton key to whatever locks together past and present.

Empedocles who put his thoughts, scientific and philosophical, into verse believed that sight was produced by a fire within the eye going forth to meet the object. What is scientifically unsound, poetry demonstrates otherwise. We light up the world with what we have. And yet, Empedocles reminds us, what we have, by way of our senses, though it seems a great deal, is not sufficient for us to grasp the whole. We require careful thought and deep reflection to get to what we cannot see.

2

Where is it is to be found, then, the combination of words that might whisk the dedicatee of this random prose to where he's never been before? I speak not so much of a geographical terrain as a mental one, an unfamiliar zone such as that into which his poetry so often takes me. Mediterranean light suffuses not the verses themselves, and this is a distinction I wish to make, but the mind that maketh them. There's no English grey in them. Their inner fire goes forth, meets its target, and the words produced tremble. I lack the critical apparatus whereby I might make a work of art more visible at a great distance, but this is not, and has never been, my chosen task. What I wish for is merely to communicate and to make good what that old pagan Libanius wrote: 'Truly it is good to speak, and to hear is better and to converse is best, and to add what is fitting to the fortunes of one's friends, rejoicing with them in some things, sorrowing with them in others, and to have the same return from them; and in addition to these there are ten thousand things in being near to one another.' And it is there again, differently garbed, in Ezra Pound's translation from the Chinese of Rihaku alias Li Po: 'What is the use of talking, and there is no end of talking, / There is no end of things in the heart.'

Allow for this sudden shift, then, from Kolymbetra to the summit of Monte Pellegrino, high above Palermo. So that you might get there, in time, move upon the sound of water dripping from the walls of a cave, which, so one is told, when dabbed to the lips, protects or even cures one. *Santuario di Santa Rosalia* is where, in 1624, the remains of the twelfth-century hermitess Rosalia or *La Santuzza* 'the little saint' were found encrusted with stalactites. After what was once her was paraded from the grotto down into Palermo and to the Cathedral they were said to have stopped the plague that was raging through the city at the time. Rosalia has since become the patron saint of the city and such is her potency still that even the young come here to pray on their knees. That parade is re-enacted every year on July 15th with an extravagance that one can't help but feel might have embarrassed her, she who shunned the public gaze.

What of Rosalia herself? There is no account of her prior to that produced by Valerius Rossi in 1590, according to which she was the daughter of Sinibald, Lord of Quisquina and of Rosa, descended from the family of Charlemagne. Aged fifteen, she fled the court purportedly to be closer to God but because nothing substantial is known about her she might have fled for reasons other. Why not, as seems most likely, the prospect of an unwelcome marriage? Women aplenty have fled would-be husbands into the arms of gods. Goethe describes the reclining golden-draped statue of Rosalia as 'so natural and pleasing, that one can hardly help expecting to see the saint breathe and move about.'

And were she to move, what then?

A story I have just read will not let go of me. At the end of Luigi Pirandello's "The Madonna's Gift" a man kneels before a statue of the Virgin, prays for the restoration to health of his one remaining daughter, the others having perished from tuberculosis, whereupon he experiences a miracle. The Virgin smiles, moves her hand, inviting him to take from it a rosary of gold and pearls, which he begins to do, when onlookers fall upon him, screaming 'Thief! Thief!,' punching him, spitting upon him, and then, ignoring his pleas of innocence, they drag him from the church into the village square where he blacks out, quite possibly dies, but not before he has a terrible vision. A shadow thrown by a tree gathers itself up into the shape of a defrocked priest whose friendship he had earlier spurned and who now laughs at him. Forgive me, I give away the end of the story but it is one which hardly anyone reads anymore. It is Pirandello at his most querulous on the nature of miracles.

A palaeontologist of some repute says Rosalia's bones may in fact be those of a goat.

Would it matter so much if they were?

Suppose, in the eyes of one of Rosalia's many devotees, maybe one as desperate as the man in the tale I've just related, she were to move just a little, and if she were seen by that person to surrender her golden filigree crown and if he were to reach for it, what then would the onlookers' reaction be? Would they not in an instant swing from piety to brute force? Outside, the stalls sell religious kitsch, kitchen aprons adorned with bare breasts and Godfather T-shirts. (This is the country where I saw in a bookshop, exhibited together, as if inseparable, two new books, one on the new pope and the other an Italian translation of *Fifty Shades of Grey*.) Away from the tackiness, through the woods that cap the mountain, a smell of wild garlic, it's where Rosalia must have wandered all those centuries ago. There is a pool nearby. Surely, all alone up here, she must have bathed sometimes, a braid snaking down her bare back.

It's an image I've taken from elsewhere.

3

THE TRAIN THAT GOES FROM Palermo to Agrigento passes through one of the world's most haunting landscapes. It stops at the station that serves both Roccapalumba and Alia. Old heart surges. A few minutes later, from the train window, it appears in the distance, the hilltop town of Alia, which my wife and I drifted into in February 1974, with no purpose other than to see what the interior of Sicily was like.

We had been advised to stick to the coast as there was nothing much to see inland. What we found was untouched by tourism, so mercifully free of it that when we walked into the village the elderly women fled into their houses and peered at us through the divides of the curtains. (Or might they not have been shutters, a friend asks me. So easily memory plays havoc with the furniture.) We had the sense of being watched from everywhere. Where would we bed down for the night? There were no hotels of any kind. We made enquiries and were directed to a handsome red-haired woman who occasionally took in strays such as ourselves. It was not a *pensione* but her home. Although I burn with shame to speak of this, and my doing so is perhaps a form of penance, our stay there would change my life. We were shown a single bed, the only one she had, and when she named the price, which was reasonable, I quibbled with her, pointing to the narrowness of the bed. A wounded look in her face, she said she really could not go any lower. We agreed to take the room because, after all, there was nowhere else to go, and it was getting late. We went for a walk and when we returned the family were at dinner, and, upon seeing us, they invited us to join them. We had a splendid feast, good red wine, followed by the woman's elderly father picking up a guitar and singing Sicilian folk tunes. All this was without charge, of course, and such was the mortification I felt at having earlier argued over the price that this single evening would transform my attitude towards travel forever. Call me a fool, but I'd sooner even be cheated a little than to question or distrust those among whom I move. What's the antonym for *swindle*? Shall I call it *grace*? Whatever it is, it's what I experienced in Alia over four decades ago.

Alia slips into the distance, and soon, the train making a curve through the hills, it is gone. It's nowhere I'll ever go back to because to do so would be to dissolve its gravitational pull and what a betrayal of one's better self that would be. Again there come lines from Middleton's poem:

> Now he says there are many places
> Not to be gone to. Memory has no desire
> To be disappointed. But, he says, nothing,
> Nothing stops you wanting to go there.

The place must be so very different now. The woman, if she lives still, I should think all the redness has gone out of her hair. And the old man, his guitar, the chords he played upon it, and his shaky voice, do they resonate somewhere in the universe? Sound, so said the physicists of old, travels forever.

4

SHAKESPEARE IN RAGUSA. *As You Like It*, the Forest of Arden transposed to where the trees become pointed spires. When I've done with Melancholy Jacques, finding in him something that is mine too, 'compounded of many simples,' I move on, with no great purpose in mind, to *Julius Caesar*, marvelling at the sheer speed of the lines, when I fall upon those in Act V, Scene I, where Cassius taunts Mark Anthony:

> Anthony,
> The posture of your blows are yet unknown;
> But for your words, they rob the Hybla bees,
> And leave them honeyless.

A passage I might have sped over at any other time here arrests me. Can this really be? A few lines from Shakespeare allude to where I just happen to be, and again I wonder how it is that so often books come to one at precisely the right moment. Maybe I should finally put to rest those hoary old notions of mine. Why should I be surprised anymore? Am I not sans teeth? I am reminded of what the poet who speaks in perfectly honed paragraphs said to me in conversation:

> Or maybe the words actually exist outside of the books and they create in the air or *against* the air such a friction that the vibratory life is drawn out of the heart of the universe and presented to you in all sorts of objective configurations which make much more of a pattern than would be available to ordinary people, who don't live among so many fricative words, words grinding away at the flesh of the universe until a huge vibratory spirit world is created. Human words, quit of the flesh, grope for the spirit, maybe?[1]

1 *Palavers: Christopher Middleton in Conversation with Marius Kociejowski* (Shearsman Books, 2004)

The old part of Ragusa where I lie, admittedly a bit tipsy from a bottle of Nero d'Avola, is called Ibla which preserves in its name a sonic memory of the ancient Hybla Hera. There are various arguments as to where the original Hybla was, but, for purposes of this prose, *this* shall be the Hybla from where the above lines from Shakespeare take their reference. I have to say it, though, I have to say that my coming across them here, in this place, confounds me. The surrounding *I Monte Ible*, the Hyblaean Mountains, are at this time of year carpeted with wildflowers, which, according to local lore, are of so powerful of scent the sniffing dogs lose their way home, and everywhere one walks one hears a steady humming of bees. How did he know, how did Shakespeare know about the Hybla bees? Could it be he walked in these very hills? I am of that barmy crowd that believes Shakespeare went to Italy, which is not quite as barmy as saying Shakespeare did not write Shakespeare, and if indeed he did go might he not have ventured further south to Sicily and there tasted of the honey that was so famous in ancient times and which was a byword for all things good and plentiful. And Shakespeare being Shakespeare, he turns the reference upside down to extraordinary effect. *Honeyless!* At about three in the morning I resolve I will honour the import of those lines and make the purchase of a jar of Hybla honey. I am not so much fanciful as I am impulsive.

I buy the *miele di carrubo*, made from the flowers of the carob tree, with its dark hint of chocolate. The honey is, in truth, a bit too grainy for my taste, crystalline, but I will consume it nevertheless because literature bids me do so. Sober now, I should have known what Shakespeare would certainly have known, that Hybla's honey was the most celebrated in the ancient world, and also that rather than make the trek here he would have read Virgil's *Eclogues* and the references they contain to the 'willow blossoms sipped by Hybla's bees' and that, as with just about everything Shakespeare saw, read and heard, it stuck with him. What did *not* stick with him? One has only to look upon the shiny globe of his forehead to see how much it contained and wanted *out* and *into* his verses. What a buzzing manufactory that mind was, a hive of memories. And then he might also have read Theocritus, a native son of Sicily, and who, in Robert Wells's modern translation of the seventh *Idyll*, speaks of how the 'snub-faced bees swarmed to the cedar hollow

> To feed the prisoner on their meadow-gathered spoil,
> Drawn in by the Muse's nectar about his lips.
> Lucky Comatas, to take such punishment,
> To be shut in a box and fed on honeycomb!

What could have possessed me to imagine I was first on the scene? And yet is it not where all great literature puts one? Who, when confronted with a great line of poetry, is not newly arrived? Who does not become its sole possessor? I see in those lines from the Roman play what no man hath seen before.

An ancient honey, the carob might be that which is referred to in the Gospels of Matthew and Mark, John the Baptist with his diet of locusts and wild honey. Some early biblical commentators took the locusts to be an allusion to the oddly shaped carob pods although probably it really was locusts he ate. They are edible, best when fried and just about manageable when raw. Did he have to pick the legs from between his teeth? And it has been suggested too that the honey he ate was actually the sap of the tamarisk tree. I'm about to fall into a jar of sticky postulates, and there, caught in the sweet goo, my arms and legs will frantically wave and kick for release. Damn it all, if Leigh Hunt did not publish his *A Jar of Honey from Mount Hybla* in 1848 but then, rather peevishly, I take comfort from the fact that the inspiration for his book was a small blue jar of Hybla honey he saw in the window of Fortnum & Mason. I got mine, sir, in situ.

On June 14, 1847, Edward Lear was walking with his companion John Joshua Proby somewhere in the *commune* of Ragusa, most probably the marvellous gorge in Ipsica that was home to the ancient Sicels who have left so few traces although they must have seemed permanent to themselves. They ghost the island's name. It was at Ipsica that a man picking lemons poured some into my knapsack. Those lemons, are they not the best anywhere, so strangely translucent in their scent and taste, as if beside them all other lemons are somehow dense? On that day in June, Lear stopped to make a pen-and-ink sketch which bears the caption: 'Hybla. P. and L. distinguish the Bees of Hybla.' The journals Lear kept in Sicily are lost, and only a book of his sketches survives, but might not he and Proby have been discussing Shakespeare's Hybla bees?

My childhood swarmed with bees. One wall of the house was colonised by them, Italian bees, I was told, famous for their good nature, and indeed, throughout all those years, not one of them ever stung me. My parents let them be. My father kept a hive not far from the house. In the winter months I would place my ear to my bedroom wall and listen to the humming within and imagined the honey dripping down between the inner and outer walls and seeping into the very foundations of the house, safe from man's sweet tooth and yet so tantalisingly close. Throughout my whole childhood that wall sang to me, and it is a kind of sonic world I carry within me still. Virgil, in his first *Eclogue*, speaks of the murmuring of Hybla bees as a lullaby for old age, and will they, I wonder, come back to me in mine. Will I cup my ear to the wall of memory? Am I not perhaps already doing so? One day, some years after I'd left home, the bees quite suddenly quit the house and my father, no superstitious man he but nevertheless one who knew his bee-lore, remarked that their departure boded ill and so it did, so it did.

And what are those lines from the poem written in the Hotel Asia Minor in Ürgüp, deep in the heart of Cappadocia? *Come, warble, come.*

> You must not cut loose from here and now,
> Both hands taking hold have to pull, he says:
> Let the crypt call to you …

5

THE MUSEO ETNOGRÁFICO PITRÈ is named after the good doctor of Palermo's poor, Giuseppe Pitrè (1841–1916), who, wanting to preserve the very soul of the people among whom he lived and worked, not only assembled a vast collection of artefacts, the majority of them contemporary, but also compiled the *Biblioteca delle tradizioni popolari siciliane*, an oral history of the island that extends to twenty-five volumes. When he treated the poor, they paid him with stories of their lives or else they told him folktales or else they gave him the lyrics and melodies of folksongs, among them, perhaps, the songs the old man in Alia played. An archaeologist of the present, there was nothing so minor he did not accord it the gravitas deserving of a people the specifics of whose lives could so easily be lost otherwise. With his interests extending to every possible area of human activity and with his mind being of a most orderly nature he singlehandedly preserved, as if in a time capsule, the social and spiritual history of a whole generation. It takes more genius to preserve the present than it does the past. Hardly known outside his native city, Giuseppe Pitrè remains one of the world's greatest folklorists.

There is a wall in the museum dedicated to ex-voto paintings, which, to my mind, are among the most touching expressions to be found in that area we call 'folk art' although even this is to employ a wobbly phrase. They belong in a place entirely their own. They are painted on small panels of wood, and contain scenes aplenty of people spewing blood, tuberculosis being then commonplace, ships imperilled at sea, a baby falling from a window or, as depicted here, a construction accident.

A saint, or the Virgin Mary herself, is at the upper corner of each of these paintings. So direct and so urgent in their import, the scholar Anna Maria Tripputi memorably describes ex-votos as an expression of faith in 'the invisible thread that links humanity to the supernatural.' Ex-voto is an abbreviated form of the Latin *ex voto suscepto* 'from the vow made' and each of these paintings is an expression of thanks given for the answering of a prayer or even, as in the case of the tumbling workmen, the briefest of invocations although more likely than not it would have been language of another kind. Are these tumbling workmen really all in the midst of prayer?

The artists (or maybe the better word is 'craftsmen') remain anonymous. Presumably they were people in the community, whose job it was firstly to have the story related to them by the relatives of the survivors or maybe even by the survivors themselves, and, secondly, to paint something approaching a likeness of the people concerned. I begin to wonder whether the painter ever questioned the miraculous aspects of the story told him but such doubt comes from the outside, where one stands at a great distance, with a cold eye, whereas to be on the inside, which is where both supplicant and painter are, is to be already deeply rooted in a mythical world where the veracity of a miracle is not as important as that world it occupies. I struggle with, and finally vanquish, the doubter in me.

Could there be, in one of their stories, the story Pirandello never wrote? I can't be sure. After all, in his *Novelle per un Anno* he wrote a story for each day of the year, only a few of which have made it into translation. What's strange, though, is how both he, this author who troubles me so, and the words of that poem continue to follow me. What did the author of the latter mean by 'This is the country of people after midnight'? The drift of it defies interpretation, and yet, if we allow it to, its meaning is clear enough, closer than language itself. Turkey may have inspired that line but it feels equally true here, and then, yes, I remember it now ... Odysseus ... but, of course! ... Odysseus knew this land. The blood that ran through his veins still runs through people's here. This, too, is a country of people after midnight. Odysseus, for surely it is he, who, in the poem, after so many centuries, has become a Muslim, saying 'May Allah lift the griefs from all of us,' and now, transposed, he has become a Christian, although maybe a doubting one. Could it be he who took a brush to one of those strange paintings so that God might here, too, 'lift the griefs from all of us?

> A Christ of Sorrows stands alone, his face
> Preserved in the original paint. That the face,
> He says, illuminates all memory of the house,
> Once you have been there, for your lifetime,
> Is not certain.

6

ARE THESE SKETCHES NOT, to paraphrase Pirandello, disconnected pieces in search of a theme? Empedocles, and who knows for sure whether he was a doctor or a charlatan, said the whole cannot be grasped except in moments of reflection when, through the power of imagination, one sees a thing from all sides. It's what poetry most wants to do, to be everywhere at once. The latest word on the *via* is that Empedocles did not plunge into the mouth of Etna, and, as if to heap disappointment upon disappointment, the story of his golden sandal being spewed up by the god he had become, from deep within the volcano, is thought to be a fabrication too. One of Empedocles' more recent biographers, a little wanting for humour perhaps, suggests that the mouth of the volcano would have been too hot for him to get close to. Among the many accounts of his death is one that he fell from a carriage, broke his thigh, and died soon after. So mundane, would this have inspired Hölderlin to compose his lines on Empedocles, Matthew Arnold his?

Sicily is full of wonders. There is the baby female Jesus, for example, which the Vatican spent many decades trying to suppress, and no, this is not some newfangled feministical notion but a nod in the direction of Persephone, she who goes into the Underworld and returns. I did go looking for her, the female Jesus said to be in a number of churches, her privates now covered by decree, but I have no report to make. For now, within the space of this prose, and with respect to the poet whom I salute, it is the Gardens of Kolymbetra that lay the most powerful claim to my imaginative sympathies.

And that poem, *that* poem:

Ah yes, he says,
Ah yes, this is the country of people after midnight;
Few have spelled out into the pleasure of a heartbeat,
Into a knot of mind, once and for all,
The loops of light they see spreading at sunrise,
The braid that snakes down a girl's bare back.

The Saddest Book I'll Never Write

And, beauty dead, black chaos comes again.
                              –Shakespeare, *Venus and Adonis*

THE OTHER NIGHT I DREAMED of Paolo. A dream more linear than most and as such more easily filed in the memory, it went something like this: my wife and I were driving through some very remote part of Syria, an area as yet untouched by the conflict. Why we were there at such a ghastly time in the country's history is unanswerable, but then dreams are not much interested in explaining mysteries. Curiously the dream was in monochrome: I always dream in colour. The sky in it was a burnished metallic grey, quite unlike any grey one finds in nature although at times London comes close. One could almost tap the end of one's pencil upon such skies.

'We are low on petrol,' my wife said.

She was at the wheel. I don't drive.

'Yes,' I replied, 'and I'm desperate for a loo.'

We pulled into a small hamlet of several buildings outside one of which was a rusty petrol pump. I got out of the car to investigate. (Hereafter, my wife disappeared from the dream.) I knocked at the door of the building closest to the pump but there was no response nor were there any signs of life from the neighbouring houses. I might have been prowling a ghost village. Suddenly I was aware of a sound of singing from a nearby, rather squat, stone building. I walked towards it and stepped inside a hall densely packed with people singing a hymn. After they stopped there came from the front a priest's voice. It was so crowded I couldn't see above people's heads but the Arabic-speaking voice, so mellifluous, so dramatic in its quiet tone, which, one suspects, has more than an element of artifice in it, was unmistakeably his.

I waited for an appropriate lull in the proceedings.

'Father Paolo,' I cried out, 'we are short of petrol and I'm in need of a toilet.'

There was silence, then an audible ripple in the congregation of someone trying to squeeze through. The figure of Paolo emerged from the wall of people, not the burly man so familiar to me but a skeletal figure, horribly emaciated, his hair grown, beard unruly. It was him and it was *not* him.

'You are alive!' he exclaimed.

Tears rolled down his cheeks as he embraced me.

'On the contrary,' I replied, '*you* are alive.'

'Yes, but it's *your* name on the list of those to be killed.'

I awoke, greatly stricken.

Father Paolo dall'Oglio was taken captive on July 29, 2013, in ar-Raqqah, by the very people whom he'd gone to see in order to negotiate the release of hostages. They were members of the Islamic State of Iraq and Syria (ISIS), an al Qaeda affiliate by far the most ruthless in the region. It was the first I'd heard of them. A year later, there was nobody who didn't feel a chill at the mention of their name, whose latest manifestation is Islamic State. So ghastly they were, so unreasonable, that even al Qaeda has put them at a distance. Suicidal might be one word used to describe Paolo's presence there, and indeed I have heard it said from someone else who'd met him a couple of times that it might have been, from his side, a craving for martyrdom. I think it was neither and that his self-confessed vanity, immense popularity and quick wit were such that he felt himself invincible. Only hours before his capture he gave a public speech in which he called for an end to the violence against Kurds and it may have been this that sealed his fate. (There has been within the bigger conflict another, equally brutal, between Islamists and Kurds.) An early report had it that he was strangled in his cell, a later one that he'd been shot, and yet another that he was being kept alive for purposes of negotiation. Another, more recent, rumour would have us believe he had been sighted but this, like all the others, is unsubstantiated. I am yet to be convinced that Islamic State, especially if they are 'outsiders' and not privy to the affection Paolo inspired in Syrian Muslims and Christians alike, would be sophisticated enough to recognise his bartering value. Surely, if he were still alive, some signal would have been made by now. Surely, if he were dead, the body of so large a man would have been found. All these months later, in my thoughts, I have buried and resurrected Paolo at least a dozen times. So often I've been wrong in my gloomy prognostications about other things and so I gamble a little: I pronounce him dead so that he might live.

Over the years since I first met him, when I so clumsily blundered into his life, and then later devoted a chapter to him in my book *The Street Philosopher and the Holy Fool*, Paolo had become an increasingly important presence in Syria, perhaps the one figure of unity upon whom, in imagination at least, might be built some vision of a reconstructed future. I fear solidarity is precisely what is not wanted by his captors. A man temperamentally incapable of neutrality on any issue, Paolo openly criticised the Syrian regime while at the same time calling for a peaceful democratic transition or what he called 'consensual democracy.' Warnings, none of which he heeded, were issued against him. After he presided over services for the murdered Christian filmmaker, Bassel Shehadeh, the regime called for his expulsion. This he also ignored, going about his business as usual. When, in May 2012, he wrote an open letter to the UN peace envoy, Kofi Annan, he was persuaded or, rather, he was forced by the church hierarchy (which, it is rumoured, acted in collusion with the regime) to leave the country. Clearly he did so unwillingly: 'It would be better for me to be dead with the martyrs of this country,' he said, 'than to go away in exile.' On June 12, 2012, upon hearing of his expulsion, the Syrian populace, or, rather, that part of it which stood against the regime, declared a "National Paolo Day". Some Christians, mindful of their own physical welfare, disassociated themselves from him. The greater part of the following year he spent travelling worldwide, calling for international action in the face of the spiralling crisis, saying that a failure to do something would result in the rise of extreme Islamist groups. During this period he had made clandestine visits back into the so-called 'free zone' of Syria where his fears would be proven all too accurate.

When I last visited the monastery of Deir Mar Musa, in 2008, Paolo was away on business in Damascus and there was no certainty I would get to see him this time. I had made a poor start with one of the monks, Boutros, who was quite hostile to my presence and as if to underline his antipathy towards me, when he showed me my sleeping quarters, a dormitory of empty beds, he positioned me directly above the toilet on the floor below. My wife, in the women's quarters, fared rather better. Boutros is famously combative, at times perverse in the extreme, a football fanatic to boot, and as such this has made him into something of a protected species. The greatest love afforded such people is to let them be. At least I think that was the monastic take on him. I suspect he was a necessary ingredient, an unruly mascot of sorts, a measure against which others might take their own spiritual bearings.

My wife and I were sitting on the floor of the chapel, observing the hour's silence that is held prior to Mass, a silence held in the middle of desert silence, a silence as profound as any I have experienced, a silence such as stirs one's spiritual recesses. The service was just about to begin when suddenly Paolo came through the door and, spotting me, hugged me. I caught out of the corner of my eye Boutros's glowering face.

Boutros is presently one of only five people to have remained in the monastery. Already the place, which is so remote, has been raided twice by masked gunmen. May Allah protect him, protect Sister Huda and whoever else is there.

I HAVE ONLY SCANT NEWS of other people close to me.

Darayya is a town on the outskirts of Damascus and it is said to be where on 'the Damascus road' the Apostle Paul had his conversion. It is where Sulayman lived when I last saw him, his neighbours mostly farmers, congenial people. He described Darayya as a haven where the ways of life were simple and one could breathe fresh air. I'm sure it was not quite as simple as Sulayman claimed because farmers are never simple nor was the air quite as fresh as he would have me believe, but it was where he flourished. Alchemy was still his first love, although now more quietly pursued than before, and he was also the proud owner of a dump truck with which he became a free-lance garbage collector. A man not ecologically sound in his thinking, he would burn piles of rubbish outside his house, a mountain of plastic shavings once, which, much to the annoy-ance of his neighbours, blanketed the area with blue smoke. The pollution he made was far worse than the pollution he sought to disperse. One day he got into a row with one of his clients who flung a bag of garbage at him, which missed and hit Sulayman's helper instead. Sulayman, always one to exact revenge, later backed his truck against the entrance of the other man's house, and tipped out the contents, sealing his foe inside. We who heard his stories, which he told without a flicker of a smile, rolled about in mirth because this was the same man who, in similar voice, would expound on the great mediaeval mystic Ibn al-'Arabi. One never knew what one got next with him and this, his unpredictability and quicksilver mind, was his true alchemy.

Darayya is now mostly rubble.

First came the aerial bombing, then the slaughter, one of the worst to date, with regime soldiers going from door to door bayoneting and shooting the male occupants. It is said upwards of a thousand people were killed and hastily buried in long ditches. A young and pretty TV reporter, Micheline Azar, whose name I include here so that she might be preserved in some catalogue of the damned, moved nonchalantly among the dead and dying, thrusting her microphone in the faces of victims, one of whom was a small child snuggled beside the body of her dead mother. Miss Azar seemed quite unfazed. She might have been delivering sweets in a children's playground, chirping away about how these *silly, silly* people had brought all this upon themselves. The footage, shown on Syrian TV, was bizarrely accompanied by what sounded like a Hollywood movie score. All regimes ultimately damn themselves.

Some years ago, I witnessed what in legend has been described as blood falling from the skies. It was the *rīh al-khamsīn* ('the wind of the fifty') that brings sand from the Sahara and which, when combined with rainfall, produces a reddish appearance. A thin layer of red sand covered everything including a white shirt I'd washed and hung out to dry. The clouds were a sickly, rotting pink, the sun behind them a dirty white disc. I'd never seen a climatic condition that disturbed me more, which resembled the skies in the nineteenth-century English painter John Martin's apocalyptic visions. Sulayman, when I saw him later, spoke words that were prophetic in their import.

'The pink you saw was the shed blood of nations,' he told me, 'whose citizens have been unjustly killed. My wife said to me, "This is the blood of martyrs everywhere." There is to be a change, but what this change will be we don't know. I felt uncomfortable. I went into the open and started saying, "There is no God but Allah," and then I made a supplication. May God help us!'

There is no saying whether or not Sulayman lives.

Abed, when I last heard of him, was descending ever deeper into the madness that I chronicled in *The Pigeon Wars of Damascus*. According to one person who saw him not long ago, he was discussing with friends a dream in which the playwright Arthur Miller presented himself as a Sufi. They concluded it must be true. I have heard nothing of him since. There have been several street battles in the area where he lives.

Yasser, who appears briefly in *Street Philosopher* and at great length in *Pigeon Wars*, is being actively sought by the *mukhabarat*, the Syrian secret police. They have gone to where his shop is, asking neighbours after his whereabouts. God forbid he should ever fall into their hands. A friend of his was tortured to death by them and before dying gave out names and addresses of people, Yasser's included, whose 'crime' was that they had taken part in the very first peaceful protests calling not for regime change but for greater liberties. Later, on another rally, he witnessed a fellow protester set upon by government-sponsored thugs with iron bars who beat him to death. The thugs or *shabiha* (which translates as 'ghosts') were themselves at the point of a gun. Yasser fled and spent some hours in a cemetery, weeping and clinging to a tombstone, the dying cries of the other man still in his ears. Later, he was imprisoned in a cell so packed with people there was room enough for only one person at a time to lie down for an hour's rest. After his release, still early days in the conflict, he ran money and medicine to the besieged city of Homs, an act punishable by death. Still later, after working in a refugee camp on the Syrian-Turkish border, he singlehandedly set up a field hospital near Hama, at one point a missile landing close to the vehicle in which he was transporting an X-ray machine he'd smuggled in from Turkey. As of late, and far from his home, he has suffered a tragedy of the kind that afflicts so many people in exile, for whom not only their material but also their familial worlds dissolve. One day those tragedies will need to be chronicled too.

Yasser tells me a story that is almost unbearable in its poignancy. His elderly parents who live in a part of Damascus that has been subjected to numerous air attacks by the regime concocted a plan to visit Yasser's brother who lives in exile in Lebanon, which by car is only a couple of hours' distance. The expense of getting there was close to prohibitive, however, and so his mother sold her jewellery so as to enable the journey. She and their husband borrowed their daughter's car, and when they arrived at the border the Syrian officials checked their documents. Yasser's mother was given permission to go through but not his father who many years before had been imprisoned by the regime. An old man and lame, he still bore the black mark that not even recent, bigger, events could wash away. He urged his wife to go ahead, saying not to worry about him, that he would find his way back to Damascus on his own, and she said no, she would always remain at his side. And so they both returned to Damascus all the poorer in purse but richer in marriage.

I thumb through the pages of my two Syrian travelogues, wondering about other people and what has happened to them. Abu Walid, old codger, spinner of fabulous stories, both Montgomery's and Hitler's confidante, has probably been spared all this. When on my last visit I looked for him the carpet sellers on a Street Called Straight told me he had not been seen for some time. A year before, Abu Walid, spluttering with theatrical rage, told me that he had gone to the British Embassy to lodge a complaint against me, saying I'd made £1,000,000 from my book, which contained a chapter about him, and that he was demanding his share. When I asked him what he felt I should give him as compensation he answered that it was between Allah and myself to determine, in which case, I answered, if Allah sets His seal upon the figure it was not for him to argue against it. Abed who was with me at the time said it was a good response. I pressed something rather less than a million in his hand, double what I normally gave him, and not too far short of what I actually made on the book. I was thanked with a sour olive grimace.

As for Our Lady of Soufanieh such news as I have is that Myrna still thrives, suspended between kitsch and moral rectitude. I am, with respect to the religiosity that surrounds her, no calmer in my unease. I would never, on the other hand, speak a word against her for she is in her faith absolutely true and of the stigmata with which she is afflicted or graced there are witnesses aplenty.

The man from whom I bought a chapbook of Shaykh Ahmad al-Harun's miracles, at a table at the end of the Souq Hamadiye, at the entrance opposite the Umayyad mosque, where he sold his religious books, was killed by a stray missile.

The Prince of Fools, where's he? Abu al-Talib, where now his magnificent nose?

Sometimes what brings the horror home to me is not the televised human carnage but, rather, news of the destruction of a single familiar place. I am thinking about Yasser's crooked little house in the old city of Damascus, where I stayed the last few times. This is not to say I think less of people than I do of buildings but that with the latter what is taken away with them is the patina of continued human existence. I will go further and say that the tearing apart of a country's historical heritage makes it all that much easier to take innocent lives. I loved Yasser's house. I imagine the very air where it once stood aches. So contorted it had become over the centuries, its wooden beams bending this way and that, it boasted not a single right angle. While lying awake at night, listening to the passers-by below, one could discern in the ringing of their footsteps the tonal difference between that produced by shoes upon stone and upon concrete. One day, in June 2013, several streets away, just off the Street Called Straight, a suicide bomber blew himself up, taking with him, so diabolically without purpose, another four lives. Although the explosion did relatively little damage to the buildings in the immediate vicinity the fluke of it was that the only building to collapse was several streets away, Yasser's house. It virtually spilled into the alleyway. When Yasser told me the news I couldn't sleep that night for thinking of its delightful features and how it had made me feel close to the centre of two millennia of mercantile existence.

THE SADDEST BOOK I'LL NEVER WRITE is one in which I return to Syria to enquire after those about whom I wrote earlier. While I hope a repeated serving of this volume[1] will be a reminder of a world all but gone what it describes was already mostly gone by the time I began work on the subsequent volume, which is to say a few years before the current horrors. What was so alive for me during the writing of the first book was already by the time it hit the shelves on the wane. Something I should have had the wit to include in it is a snippet of conversation I had with Abed in 1996. Almost two decades later, I remember it vividly as if what was being offered me then was some prefiguration of what was to come. We were standing against the wall of a building on the east side of Marjeh Square where, a few feet above our heads, jutting out from a wall, was a small dusty satellite dish. What

---

1 The present writing was designed to be the Introduction to a new edition of *The Street Philosopher and the Holy Fool* (Eland, 2015). It was not used by the publishers, perhaps rightly so, for fear it might cloud that book's azure.

was it doing there? At that point people were not allowed to own private satellite dishes. It appeared to be out of use or perhaps it never was in use or maybe it was some kind of surveillance device.

Abed pointed to it and said, '*That* is our future. Our world will change.'

When I wrote *Street Philosopher* there were no mobile phones, no computers and no satellite dishes. Five years later, as if to make up for lost time, these things were in abundance, almost exaggeratedly so. One could stand on the roof of any building in Damascus and see the mushrooming of satellite dishes. Computers, for those who could afford them, had become commonplace and there were even internet cafés. It was no longer possible to hold a conversation without continual interruptions from a mobile phone and even at restaurant tables calls were continually being taken or made. I met a man with two mobiles. 'One for the wife,' he joked, 'the other for the mistress.' A couple of years later, as if what the human race needed most was to immunise itself against depth and silence, flat-screen televisions were mounted on the walls of most restaurants, their presence so jarring against the simple beauty of the black-and-white (*ablaq*) stone walls. What was already commonplace elsewhere in the world seemed all the more intrusive here. It was as though the very social engine that drives a people as a whole had been speeded up faster than the senses could absorb. What it meant on another level, of course, was that Syrians were no longer isolated from the outside world. The Arab Spring would not have been possible without the gadgetry that people first took to in order to amuse themselves.

The following passage is from *Pigeon Wars* and it still feels true:

> When I first met Abed and Sulayman it was at just the right moment in our respective histories, which is to say it required their being the precise ages they were, when they

could still entertain hopes for the future, and my being the age I was, a couple of decades older, when I could see just far enough behind me to fathom there might be difficulties for them in store and so I could tremble for them a little. I could also partake in their youthful dance. The visions of youth, the wilder they are the less supportable, and this is especially true of young people in the Middle East where not much legroom is available. It's not the sun alone that so quickly ages them. Also it required Damascus being at a critical juncture in its history, when there was still such a thing as Arabic Time, when, as yet untroubled by computers, satellite dishes and mobile phones, its mental spaces were sufficient to allow for uninterrupted human discourse. Adjust any of the above and the first book I wrote would not have been possible. The conditions were *just so*. Already certain things I described then as commonplace, such as seeking one's counsel from fools in the street, have become rare. Whither goes the fool one no longer requires? Modernity has done much to embarrass people out of such niceties, and what they felt comfortable with yesterday today becomes fearsome. That my book would soon be somewhat antiquated did not unduly bother me. At least I'd caught the bird in mid flight, so to speak, before it settled into World Time.

What more can I say on the matter of Arabic Time?

A decade ago, I was wandering through the souq when a young Saudi in pure white called to me from inside a shop, 'Can you tell me the time, please?' I raised my wrist and he laughed out loud, 'Do you call *that* a watch?' Then he showed me his, which was made of solid gold, encrusted with jewels, and probably gave the time on the moon as well as at Fort Worth. Well, I wasn't going to let him get away with such cheek and I said to him, 'So then, do you have more time than me?' The laughter fell from his face, and he rushed over and embraced me. Would such an exchange be still possible? I think not, not now that Damascus has moved from Arabic into World Time. It was in that earlier time-frame when, no matter how painful or heavy the 'vicissi*s*itudes' of life were for them, Abed and Sulayman could still join in the dance. Certainly, as regards their society, they were out of the loop but at the same time they sought to be emblematic of all that was most precious in Damascene life, or, rather, what survived of it, the aristocracy of the broken circle.

There's one question I have to ask myself: did the conflict in Syria put an end to my relationship with the place? On one level, yes, it did, of course. Will I go back when peace of a kind resumes? I very much doubt it. Syria is a cracked vessel that will not be repaired for many decades to come. My friends have been murdered, dispersed or traumatised. I'd rather not stroll through their absence. This is a partial truth, however, and if I'm honest about it I had bid the country farewell *before* the conflict started. The sense I had was that when I first arrived in Damascus the city opened its doors to me and that with the completion of *Pigeon Wars* those same doors closed again. This takes me back to something else Abed said before we went to visit the mosque where the mystical joker Ahmad al-Harun is buried: only by going to pay my respects at his tomb would I get permission to write about Damascus and its people. It's something I've heard elsewhere, that when visiting a Muslim city in order to go *deeply* into it one must first visit its saints. There is, I think, considerable truth in this. Permission of a kind is required and it involves not just a mental surrender to what's there but also a necessary distance, a refusal to plant oneself too visibly on the scene.

I have been asked why there isn't more of *me* in my writings about Syria and the answer, quite simply, is because there would be less of everything else. I believe, too, one's character is impressed upon what one chooses to write about. One of the most important things with which one must travel is a sense of deference. Only then will there be natural sympathy with one's subjects. Also there has to be the recognition that at best one is there only on a short lease. I had a decade's grace. Again I ask the question as to whether that relationship is truly dead and the answer this time is no, of course it isn't. It survives in every conversation I have with the Syrian friends with whom I am still able to communicate. And what of Yasser's parents' failed journey to Beirut? If I were to say I am forever done with Syria, where would that leave them? They do not deserve to be stranded twice.

The other question people have asked me is *why Syria?* What can explain its hold on me? What can explain any country's hold on anyone whose country it is *not*? The more I consider the question, the more difficult any answer to it becomes. As with friendships that are close to inexplicable, so it is with certain places; it is not sufficient to say one feels at one with the landscape or with the people who occupy it; there has always got to be something more. It is almost as if one carries the gene of it inside oneself and when contact with the other is made there comes with it a form of recognition almost too deep for language. It is said by those who have been reared on Edward Said's *Orientalism* that one takes to a place a set of preconceptions and that one merely reinforces them. What I say to their wagging of fingers is that, yes, there exists in some people a predisposal to certain things and yes, one does go equipped with notions about what to expect and that yes, when met with, with the undoing of certain expectations other links are forged and, if one allows them to, they may swell into a love of place. If there is a want of fluidity or reluctance to go with the tide of what one encounters then those connections will not be made. One will be a tourist only and there are people who go as tourists throughout the whole of their lives. There must be willingness to exchange, metaphorically speaking, one's breakfast cereal for cheese and olives.

SOME PEOPLE HAVE ASKED me the meaning of the final two words of my book. *Chi anima?* They are the words I saw chiselled into the wall inside one of the monolithic tomb towers in Palmyra. I stumble a little, saying, well, there is an element of this and an element of that but really those two Italian words, so poetic in their utterance, contain within themselves a whole spectrum of possibilities. *Chi*, who … *anima*, soul … animates … 'ensouls' comes close: as one nineteenth-century sermon has it 'the Word itself became the ensouling principle.' Without wishing to sound feckless I say the phrase means *what you think it means*. Actually it is quite untranslatable and ought to be swallowed whole before the fizz goes out of it. I say, too, that when I registered those words on the wall of the tomb they seemed to be a vindication of what I had sought to achieve, which was to pin our fleeting existences to the page. I had little idea of how poignant they would one day become. They were, and continue to be, a statement not only of what *once was* but of what *not yet is*.

A writer seeks the tight knot with which he finishes a book. *The Pigeon Wars of Damascus* concludes with the image of an outdoor market hit by a bomb, and of how I had read somewhere an account of the London Blitz and how, amid the absolute destruction of several houses, a single, perfectly sound egg was seen to survive. As much as I'd like to credit myself with foresight this is not a claim I can make for myself because not even during the first days of peaceful protest in Syria did I predict the terrible outcome. At the time I had merely translated the bombings in Baghdad to Damascus. I observed how those random attacks had impressed themselves upon the minds of Syrians, some of whom said 'better our regime than what *they* have,' and when one day I strolled through that market I thought of similar markets elsewhere, where human lives were being brought to a sudden halt and for no reason at all. Somehow, though, despite my gloom (and I feel a curious sense of shame in admitting this) I had imagined all was reasonably secure.

STILL THAT DREAM won't let go of me.

I spoke to my friend Yasser who is in America now, unhappily so, who, in addition to his many other talents, is something of a dream interpreter, a stock figure in Arabic existence. I asked him the meaning of mine. Yasser, a good Muslim, has been in awe of Paolo for many years and in recent times he had assured me that Paolo was still alive. This man, he said, was too important a figure to waste. There was now a discernible shift in his tone.

'Oh,' he said gravely, 'the dream means he is no longer alive. What your dream says is that while you still require the necessities of daily existence, a toilet and petrol, Paolo is where these things no longer matter. You are among the living all of whom are on the list of those yet to die. You should draw comfort from this and the fact he is safely in another place.'

The emaciation I saw in Paolo's face, in my dream, suddenly, and most terribly, I understood it. Maybe, though, the dream means its opposite.[1]

1   Such news as there has been of Paolo's fate provides not much room for hope. According to the Syrian Observatory for Human Rights, which drew upon the testimony of an eyewitness, an ISIS defector called Abu Mohammad Assuri, Paolo was executed two hours after his detainment. It had been his third attempt to make contact with the leaders of ISIS. The first two times he was told to go away. The third attempt coincided with the arrival in ar-Raqqa of Kassab al-Jazrawi, a Saudi and one of the ISIS leaders, who had just returned from Homs where it was reported he had killed his brother. Abu Luqman, the Emir of ar-Raqqa, who knew of Paolo's high standing in the country, was away at the time. Paolo was taken into custody, accused of being an unbeliever and mocked by his captors, one of whom Paolo addressed in a manner that feels to me absolutely true to his character. When Paolo asked the age of the man and was given it he responded, saying he had read the life of the Prophet Muhammad before the other even existed. Paolo was then taken to a Sharia court in

The mystery of his disappearance has yet to be solved and it may never be, but then nor have been the fates of many thousands of people. Among them is Yasser's teenaged nephew who has not been seen for two years, who one day simply vanished into the regime's clutches. We know all too well what happened to most of those detainees. The boy's mother, close to unhinged with sorrow, would rather hear definite news of his death than be stuck inside a hell of uncertainties. If I know Paolo at all he would not want his fate to be considered at that boy's expense or at the expense of so many other people. The man truly loved his adopted country and love, when true, is a most sublime form of sacrifice. Could he really be gone? Somehow, though, whether he be alive or dead, I imagine the stunning desert and mountain landscape around Deir Mar Musa humming—yes, *ensouled*—with his presence.

---

the al-Mansoura area and after a quick trial was taken in the next room and shot fourteen times by Kassab al-Jazrawi and another man, seemingly unrelated, called Khalid al-Jazrawi, also a Saudi national. Why fourteen? Who counted? Another detail, which again seems true of the man, is that Paolo physically attacked his executioners. News of his death reached the ear of Abu Luqman who flew into a rage, and later physically attacked Kassab al-Jazrawi. After they both quietened down, they decided it would be best if Paolo's death was kept secret. Al-Jazrawi ordered his men to throw Paolo's body down a well-known geological formation in ar-Raqqa called "al-Houta," a deep hole in the earth's surface, which was used for disposing the bodies of soldiers loyal to Assad's regime. This horrifies me even more than the fact of his execution, the idea of his body hurtling through space into a place where it would be forever irretrievable. The Vatican, for want of physical evidence, which clearly it will never have, has refused to confirm Paolo's death. When warned by a friend not to take unnecessary risks, Paolo cited the words of the disciples to Jesus before he died: "Must you go to Jerusalem?" Paolo continued, "The answer is yes, sometimes you must go to Jerusalem, you must go with your physical body in order to be there." I wish, once again, against all reason, to pronounce him alive hence my putting this in a footnote.

167

Acknowledgements

THE MAJORITY OF THE PIECES in this collection were first published in *PN Review* and it is to its editor, Michael Schmidt, that special thanks are made.

"Zoroaster's Children" was first published in *Parnassus* (New York).

"A Journey to the Sun's Grave" first appeared in *CNN Traveller*.

"One Night in Marseilles" first appeared in the online magazine *Encore* (Montreal).

"The Master Calligrapher of Aleppo" first appeared in the online magazine *The Bow-Wow Shop* and was then published in *Syria through Writers' Eyes* (Eland, London, 2010, revised, enlarged edition).